MASKS

MASKS

Krystyna Baker

Texas Tech Press
Lubbock, Texas, U.S.A.
1981

ISBN 0-89672-085-3 (paper)
ISBN 0-89672-086-1 (cloth)
Library of Congress Catalog Card Number: 80:54321

Texas Tech Press
Texas Tech University
Lubbock, Texas 79409
Copyright 1981 by Texas Tech University
Printed in the United States of America

To Hershel and T. Lindsay
and Jim Broderick

Foreword

If photography's verisimilitude—its extraordinary, illusory realism—is the medium's primary means of engaging our perceptual attention, then the application of this imaging system to situations involving the visible human presence is certainly its most dependable method for seducing our emotions.

So far as I know, there are no available statistical data on the subject matter of the billions of photographs taken annually around the world. Yet it is safe to say that most of them (even in such specialized areas as medical, criminological, and scientific photography) are photographs of people. Above all else, it is people that we want to look at, people that we photograph, and people whose photographic images we hoard, annotate, preserve, restore, and pass down through the generations.

We have been doing this now for almost a century and a half. But what (if anything) have we learned collectively from looking at all these photographs of human beings? Aside from the noteworthy generalities and intriguing cultural specifics of kinesics (more loosely known as "body language"), what can we infer from these images? Many of them are—or at least aspire to be—portraits; what in fact do they portray?

Cumulatively, of course, the endless flow of photographs of people which passes before every member of our photographic culture does teach us a thing or two—or, perhaps more accurately, confirms lessons already learned. Formal portraiture, such as that of Yousuf Karsh, Philippe Halsman, and Fabian Bachrach, lets us know that the rich, famous, and powerful are still inclined to be venerated and glorified—even when that worship consists of the public presentation of Dorian Gray-style portraits such as Richard Avedon's, which record their subjects' physical decay.

As a counterbalance, so-called "candid" photography continually drives home the point that the rich and famous have moments of awkward tawdriness while the average person has unexpected moments of dignity and grace; it also reminds us that elaborate, important ceremonies can appear pointlessly inane while small, unplanned incidents can resonate with poignant prophecy. None of this is news, really; our poets, novelists, and playwrights have been telling us the same thing for hundreds of years. Democratically, however, photography provides supportive visual confirmation for almost every view of the human condition, though in and of itself it proves very little.

In a more clearly defined arena, there are the photographs of people which might be thought of as particular to each of us—that "family album," whether formally organized or not, which is composed of all the existing pictures of ourselves, our family, and friends. Certainly we turn to these for information: to see what our parents looked like on their wedding day, to find out who was present at a funeral, to verify an aunt's observation that "you have your great-grandfather's mouth."

Yet actual knowledge of the individuals behind the faces in those photographs is not a privilege conferred automatically by scrutiny of their portraits. In the right hands—that is, when placed before someone who knew intimately the subjects of a particular set of images—those photographs can be a remarkable stimulus to memory and eloquence. But place them in front of a stranger and you will find how mute they truly are.

Mute, that is, if what concerns you is "truth"—by which, in this case, I mean some verifiable correlation between one's interpretation of a facial expression and the emotional state (or general character) of the person depicted. Test this yourself by becoming the stranger just mentioned. Sit down with someone you don't know well, who has

vii

never spoken to you on matters of personal history. Take his or her family album in hand and, using the photographs as your springboard, give your impressions of the people and events depicted therein. You are guaranteed to discover in the process of doing so your own gift for fiction.

This is only to say that it is in the nature of photography to particularize—though viewers of photographs are prone to generalize from them—and that what it particularizes is the surface of things.

The deceptiveness of surfaces is a given by now; we are taught by aphorism not to judge books by their covers. Yet who among us does not gauge by appearances to some extent? The intellectual and sensory excitement unique to photography is that it entices us into a close perceptual involvement with the surface of things through its remarkable descriptive capacity, yet demands that we maintain simultaneously a rigorous sense of aesthetic distance if we are to avoid the pitfalls of personal projection and interpret each image strictly on the basis of the visual information it provides. In short, the photograph's descriptive thoroughness is so effective as to be intellectually subversive. As Leonardo once wrote, "The more minutely you describe, the more you will confuse the mind of the reader and the more you will prevent him from a knowledge of the thing described."

This is very much an issue in this sequence of Krystyna Baker's photographs, and one of which she is aware, as her preface indicates. In her photographs we are presented with frontal views of a dozen human faces, each one displaying a variety of expressions. Baker's images offer us nothing more, nothing less, and nothing else. All other information, visual and verbal, has been excluded deliberately—no captions, no biographical data, no gesture, environment, or context are offered to confirm or contradict our responses.

The consequence of this strategy is to concentrate our attention on these visages and their variations: spotlighted thus, each face becomes a stage on which an expressionist drama is played. Baker uses light and silver in a highly sculptural fashion here, emphasizing the plastic, dimensional characteristics of each of her subjects. Certainly they are particularized by her technique; could there be a more distinctively different set of faces? Yet they are, oddly, not personalized thereby. Rather, they are made to seem archetypal, iconic; they become, as Baker calls them, *masks*.

Masks (like photographs) are ritual artifacts—visually isolated moments sliced out of the flux of human expression and frozen, exaggerated, intensified by stasis. They are in that sense false—or, less judgmentally, limited—and we do not look to them for accurate and complete information on the life and character of those whom they depict.

We do look to human faces (and photographs thereof) for that information, however—even though, as Baker implies, those faces offer us nothing more than a succession of masks, no more reliable than graven ones though they're made of living flesh, skin, and bone. What do we know of these people from these photographs? What countries are they from? What have they seen, and missed? What have been their triumphs and defeats? Is that old man savoring a sweet memory or reliving his deepest grief? Is that young women devious, or rather impish? That questions such as these are irresistible is, in itself, a revelation. That these images by themselves—whether taken singly or even in sequences—offer no dependable answers whatsoever is very much the point.

Thus this book joins the company of a number of photographic works which are not about portraiture as such but rather about the human face and our complex relationship to it. I am thinking here of a diverse group: Charles Darwin's *The Expression of the Emotions in Man and Animals*, a study in the artificial simulation of facial expression by the application of electrodes, with its marvelous images by O. G. Rejlander and a "Dr. Duchenne"; Ralph Eugene Meatyard's *The Family Album of Lucybelle Crater*, which contrasts faces and masks in an exploration of shifting identities; Athena Tacha's *Facial Expressions I*, a broadside in which the range of the artist's own facial gestures is recorded; Lucas Samaras' *Samaras Album*, a suite of several hundred "autopolaroids" in which the artist acts out the many facets of his own persona; and Ken Ohara's *One*, which bombards the viewer with so many faces that it gradually reveals just how little information—even about such basic matters as gender—can be extracted from photographs of the human visage.

This book merits inclusion in that group, certainly; and yet that is only one way to approach, interpret, and respond to it. Yes, it is intellectually provocative, and relevant to the iconic studies of art historians, anthropologists, and others. Looked at another way, however—as an extended and carefully organized sequence of images by a thoughtful and articulate photographer—this book becomes something quite different. Think of it as a soundless dream, a vision—or what you see in your mind's eye as you come out of the ether. This peculiar succession of faces—all ages, races, and sexes—alternately receding and advancing, expressions constantly changing (but sometimes recurring) . . . they seem to be on the verge of telling us something, seem in fact to have messages to deliver. Their lips shape words we will never hear, their frowns and smiles inflect inaudible sentences.

On this level the book becomes an act of the imagination, with an almost cinematic structure: it has rhythms and tempos, pacing and movement. Scale and juxtaposition are employed adroitly, yet never obtrusively; even if we stop to admire the craft involved in their making, these images always return us to their subjects, the faces, the masks. That they seem by and large benign—or, at least, not overtly threatening—is small consolation. Their muteness is what creates our compelling urge to add a soundtrack, to project personal histories upon them, to put words in their mouths. What we want to know—and what Baker makes clear we will never, in any case, know—is: Who is behind all this?

A. D. Coleman
Staten Island, New York
October, 1980

CONTENTS

Preface

For many years, I have been fascinated with photographs of human faces. Wherever I have gone, I always have stopped by photographers' studios and gazed at the photographs of the people who had looked into cameras and now looked back at me. I remember such an occasion at a small 1930's studio in my home town of Łodz, Poland. It was a dark and quiet night and the shop window was brightly lit. I looked at all those people whom I didn't know—embracing brides and grooms, girls in white first-communion dresses, men with short hair from the army, teenage girls with teased hair and heavy makeup. . . .

When I became a photographer, the fascination with human faces started to be even stronger. I was interested in eyes, the movement of lips, whiskers and smooth skin, straight and crooked teeth, but I realized that they did not contribute to our knowledge about the inner character and emotions of the persons. As Duane Michals stated, "Most portraits are lies. People are rarely what they appear to be. To interpret wrinkles as character is insult, not insight." [Duane Michals, *Real Dreams* (Danbury: Addison House, 1976), 2.]

Once I realized that photographic portraits were only skin deep, my photography of human faces turned to the treatment of faces as masks. We all wear masks, many different masks—one for the boss, one for the lover, one for the mirror, one for the camera. George Santayana stated similarly:

> Masks are arrested expressions and admirable echoes of feelings, at once faithful, discreet, and superlative. Living things in contact with the air must acquire a cuticle, and it is not urged against cuticles that they are not hearts; yet some philosophers seem to be angry with images for not being things, and with words for not being feelings. Words and images are like shells, no less integral parts of nature than are the substances they cover, but better addressed to the eye and more open to observation. [George Santayana, *Soliloquies in England* (New York: George Scribner's Sons, 1922) 131-132.]

There are many reasons for us to wear masks—sociological, psychological, cultural. The whole of civilization controls what is accepted and what is not. Society dictates what kind of face we are supposed to "wear" to church or a social meeting: what kind of photographs we are supposed to have made when we graduate, get married, or die. We can draw a parallel between life and drama, with the same devices used in the theater: actors, stages, audience, scripts, and masks.

The dichotomy between the inner reality (emotions and feelings) and the visual presentation (facial expressions) is one of my main concerns. What is visual laughter can be mental pain; what is visual pain can be mental laughter. The masks we wear frequently hide our true emotions and feelings.

On the other hand, however, the faces-masks have their own visual lives. There are so many people with terrific, strong faces, I have found myself constantly searching for more. Wherever I go I look at people and quite often I get strange looks back. These people wonder why I look so intently at them and they try to remember where they have met me before. I have to make a decision at the very moment I see them for I probably will never see them again.

On one occasion I was looking for the face of an old Mexican lady. My doctor's nurse who was Mexican said that she had a great-grandmother who was half-Indian and half-Mexican. The lady was eighteen when she came to Texas from Mexico, and she was so beautiful that she was shown in county fairs as an "Indian Princess." She is in her eighties now and she is still a georgeous woman—a true Indian princess.

Another time I managed to get an introduction to an old Black lady. I came and found her on her porch, sitting in an old armchair. On every visit after that, I found her sitting in the same spot. We never entered the house because obviously the walls were too confining for her. This feeling of confinement became so acute at times that she would run away from her house and her son. She would set off on foot in the morning and walk for miles, not returning until she was ready to face it again.

I was meeting people whom I otherwise would never have met. The camera is a *carte blanche* for knowing people. Diane Arbus said:

> If I were just curious, it would be very hard to say to someone, "I want to come to your house and have you talk to me and tell me the story of your life." I mean people are going to say, "You're crazy." Plus they're going to keep mighty guarded. But the camera is a kind of license. A lot of people, they want to be paid that much attention and that's a reasonable kind of attention to be paid. [*Diane Arbus* (Millerton, N.Y.: Aperture, 1972), 1].

Before making any of these photographs, I talked with each person, usually for several hours. I asked about them, about their lives. My deep interest in "who they were" fascinated the people. They saw me as an exotic visitor from another world who saw beauty in them and their lives. They reached out to me and talked. I opened up and talked too. The distance between us dissolved and we touched.

While we talked the presence of the camera built an excitement and tension between us. We did not know exactly what would happen—an element of the unknown was always there.

When I made the photographs I found myself under such emotional tension that my hands were trembling and I could not keep the camera steady. At the time I was so excited that part of me became part of my people. I would exclaim, "Oh yes, yes, you are great, hold it, hold it." The moments were so enchanting and hypnotic that they became for me timeless. I never knew how long it took—it could have been moments or maybe hours.

The camera seemed almost a burden in such moments: remembering ASA, focusing, and advancing film. But the desire to keep the magic time forever makes a photographer possessive. We want to have a thin piece of film to preserve the past.

Till the negatives are developed and contact prints are done, I always feel like a pregnant woman—worried. What will they look like? Will they be healthy? So many things can go wrong that I am never absolutely sure until the actual prints are made.

Printing is completely different from photographing. Some people say that it is mechanical, but I never found anything mechanical about printing. True, it is a different experience, but it is equally emotional for me. The darkroom has its own rituals. When I photographed I was with people, but printing requires isolation, seclusion. You are all by yourself. You expose the paper and put into the developer. You agitate the paper as you would rock a baby—slowly and gently. You pull your fingers across the paper in a caress and you feel the developer flow through your fingers. Your eyes become as a wildcat's; you notice every highlight and shadow in the semidarkness. The image appears in front of you and each time it is a miracle. The ritual continues—shortstop, fixer. Then you turn on the light to see what you have.

Every photographer has a mental image of an ideal photograph. The actual photographs are better or worse, but never as we imagine them to be. It is part of the strength and magic of photography.

This concept of the ideal image can be carried further to the credibility of the image:

> People believe in photographs. Whatever their response may be to sculptures, etchings, oil paintings, or woodblock prints, and regardless of the level of sophistication they bring to encounters with such works, people do not think them credible in the way they do photographs. [A. D. Coleman, "The Directorial Mode: Notes toward a Definition," (*Artforum*, XV, No. 1, September 1976), 55.]

According to Coleman the following are reasons for the credibility of photography:

1. Photography employs Renaissance perspective scientifically and mechanically.
2. Photography, by using an optical/chemical relationship, has the built-in lack of aesthetic distance.
3. The mechanical or nonmanual aspect of photography (as is not the case in painting or drawing) causes an absence of syntax.

In other words, belief in photography comes from "concretized seeing," and seeing is believing. But Buckminster Fuller points out that, " 'Seeing is believing' is a blind spot in man's vision." The mechanical treatment of perspective is distorted. Aesthetic distance can be achieved in photography through choice and omission. In spite of its mechanical aspect, photography, like the other visual arts, can have syntax through the compilation of visual signs.

Photography carries with it additional restrictions which viewers readily accept. The size of the photographed object is drastically reduced. Black and white photography lacks the colors of the real world. The representation of an object is static and surface. We cannot look from behind or from the sides. The rectangular frame rigidly prevents us from making any further investigation.

In spite of all these restrictions, photography is a medium that we believe. Photography is a source of information about people, events, places. It completely revolutionized tourism; we no longer go to see strange and unknown places, rather we go to compare the real place with what we already know from photographic images.

In literature a poet or novelist no longer gives detailed descriptions of places and people. He turns instead to the psychic dialogue of the human mind encompassing inner feelings and thoughts. In painting, artists have turned toward the inner process of creativity to give us abstract art; they have used photography as a mimetic tool in Photo Realism.

Photography not only presents reality (distorted or not), but it also can create a new level of reality. Then, like the other visual arts, photography can have aesthetic distance and syntax. The directorial mode (setting up the photographed subject), unlike the photojournalistic style, enables the artist to control the photographed image as well as to create a collection of signs that have syntax. The mode also enables the artist to produce through elimination and inclusion a greater aesthetic distance than does photojournalism.

The directorial mode provides the photographer control of the photographed subject. Dealing with human faces, I include certain parts of the face and exclude others; specifically, I exclude hair, ears, and neck. The arrangement of the face is always frontal and on the same level as the camera lens. The image of the face is enclosed within a rectangle or square then placed on a white, or occasionally a black, background. The visual order and clarity of such arrangement serves to counterbalance the emotional side of photographing itself.

Usually I work in series. Series always have greatly interested me; the images of the faces are sometimes similar to each other, with only minute changes. The viewer has to make a mental comparison and contrast between them. The individual images also produce motion as if the photographs were individual frames on motion picture film.

The frames of faces-masks stopped in space and time are counterparts of studio portraits. They are to be taken for what they are—beautiful masks—our masks. What we feel inside is our happiness and trauma—our mutual human mystery.

Krystyna Baker

3

SALLY

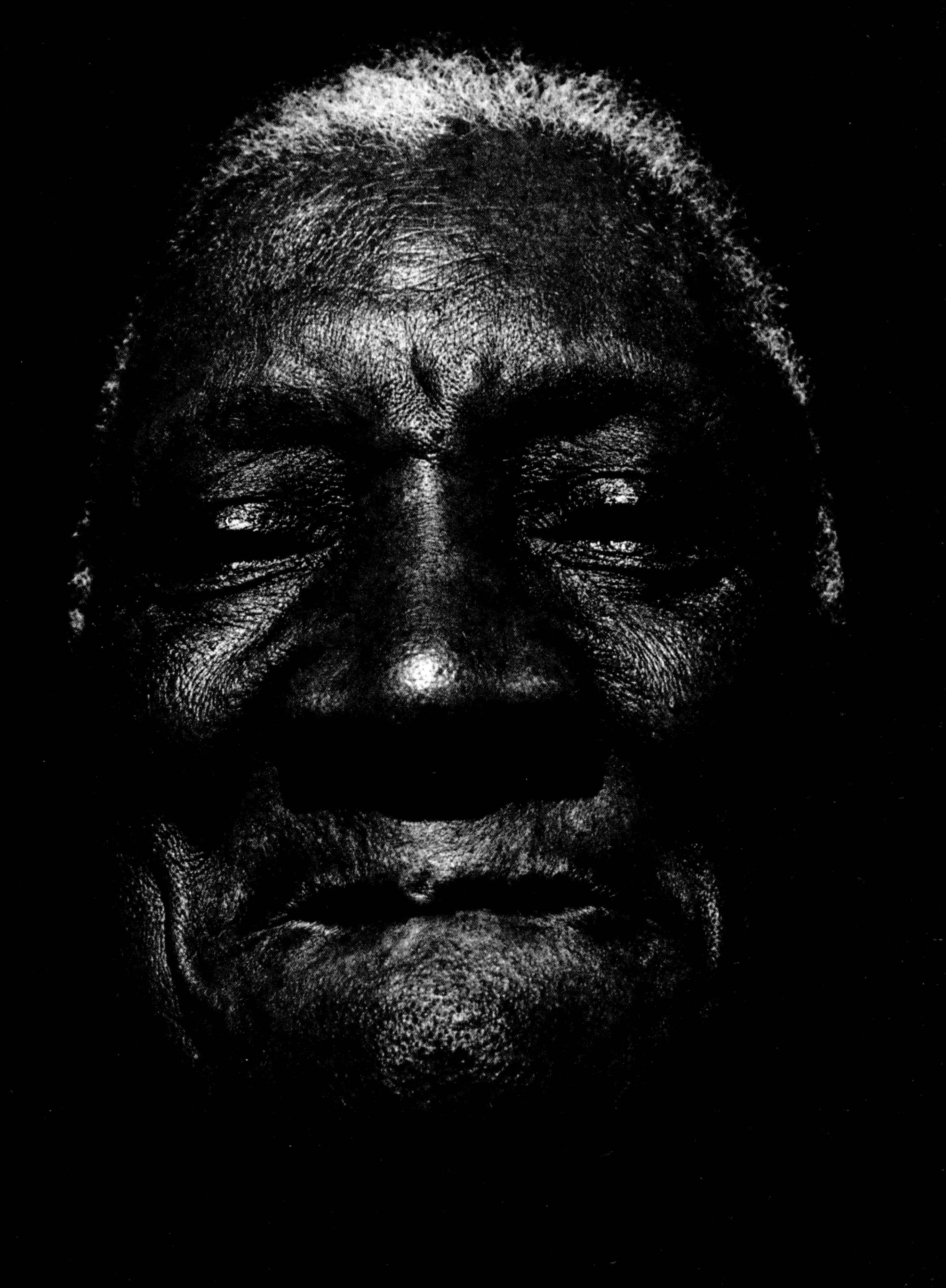

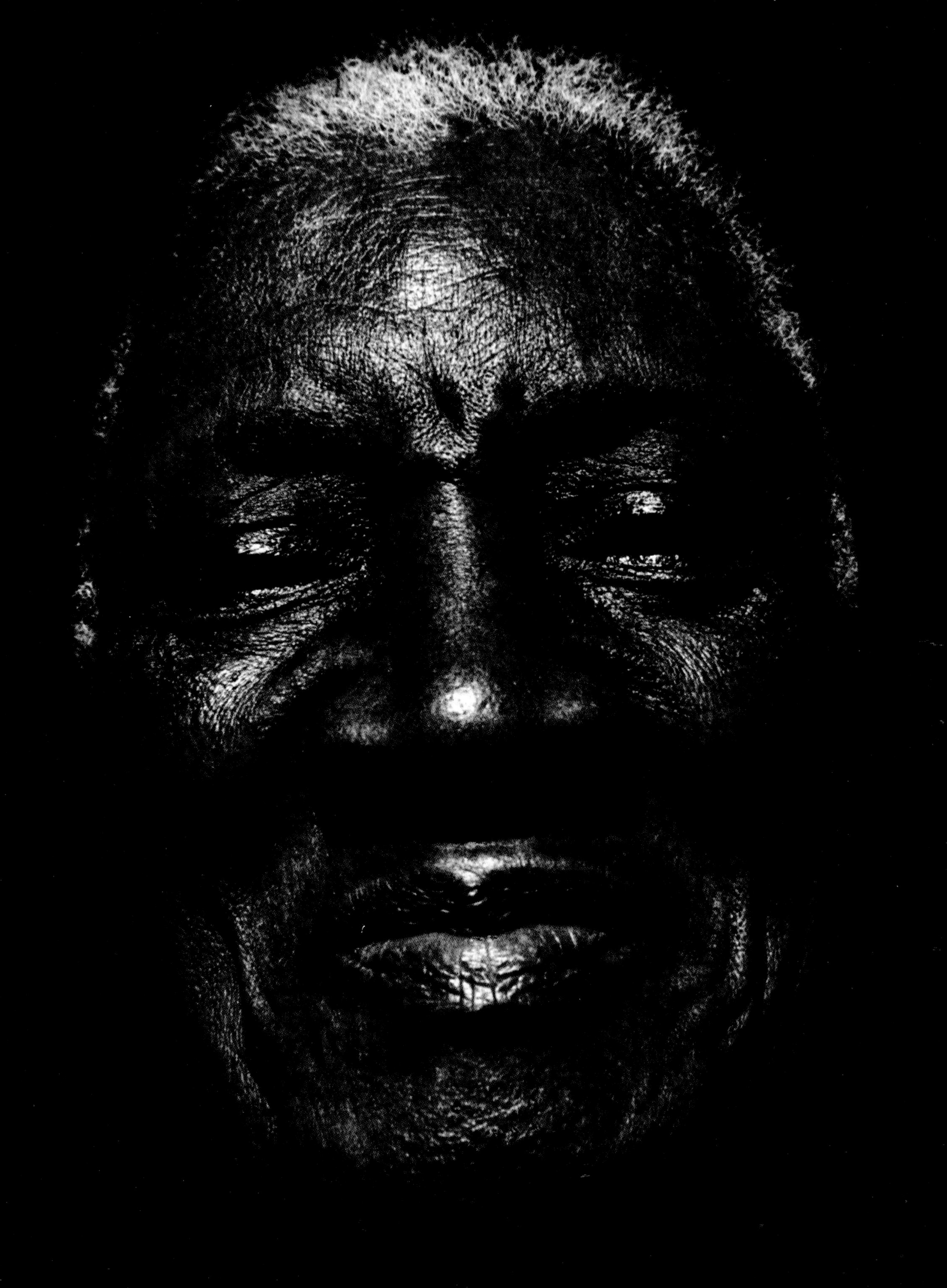

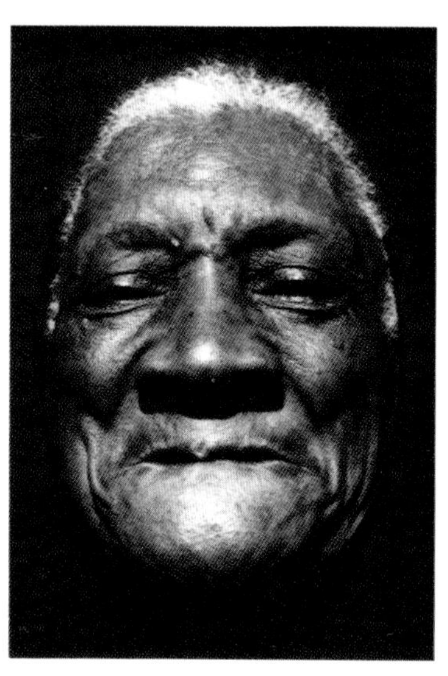

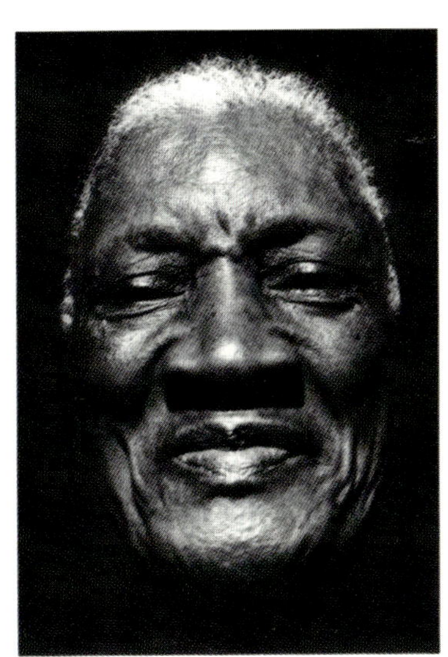

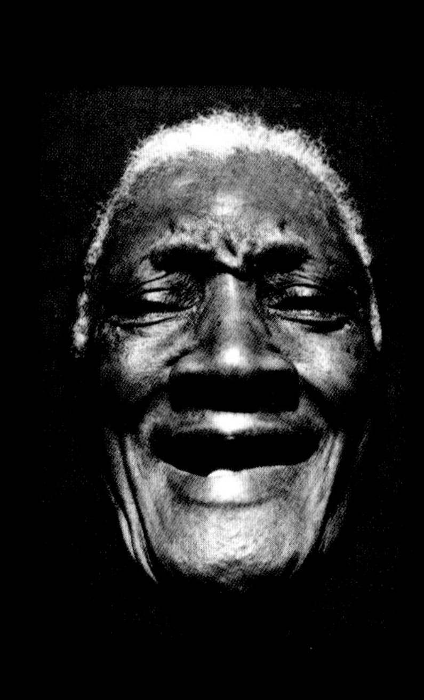

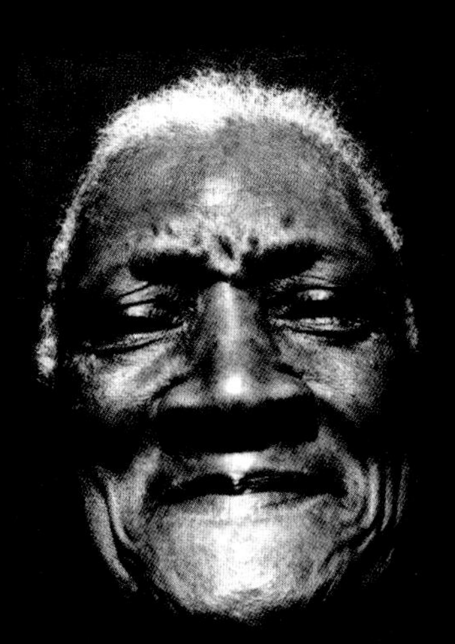

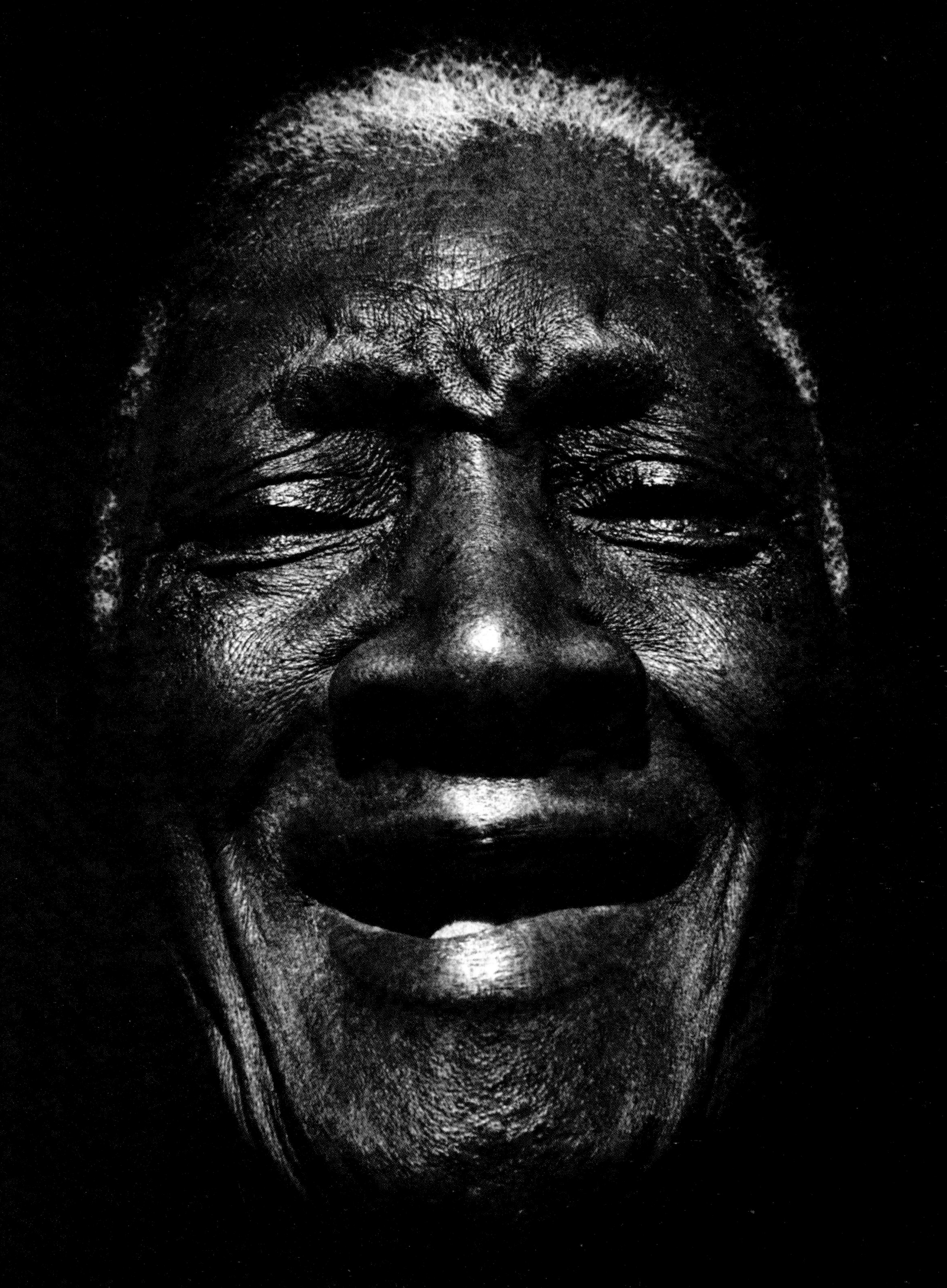

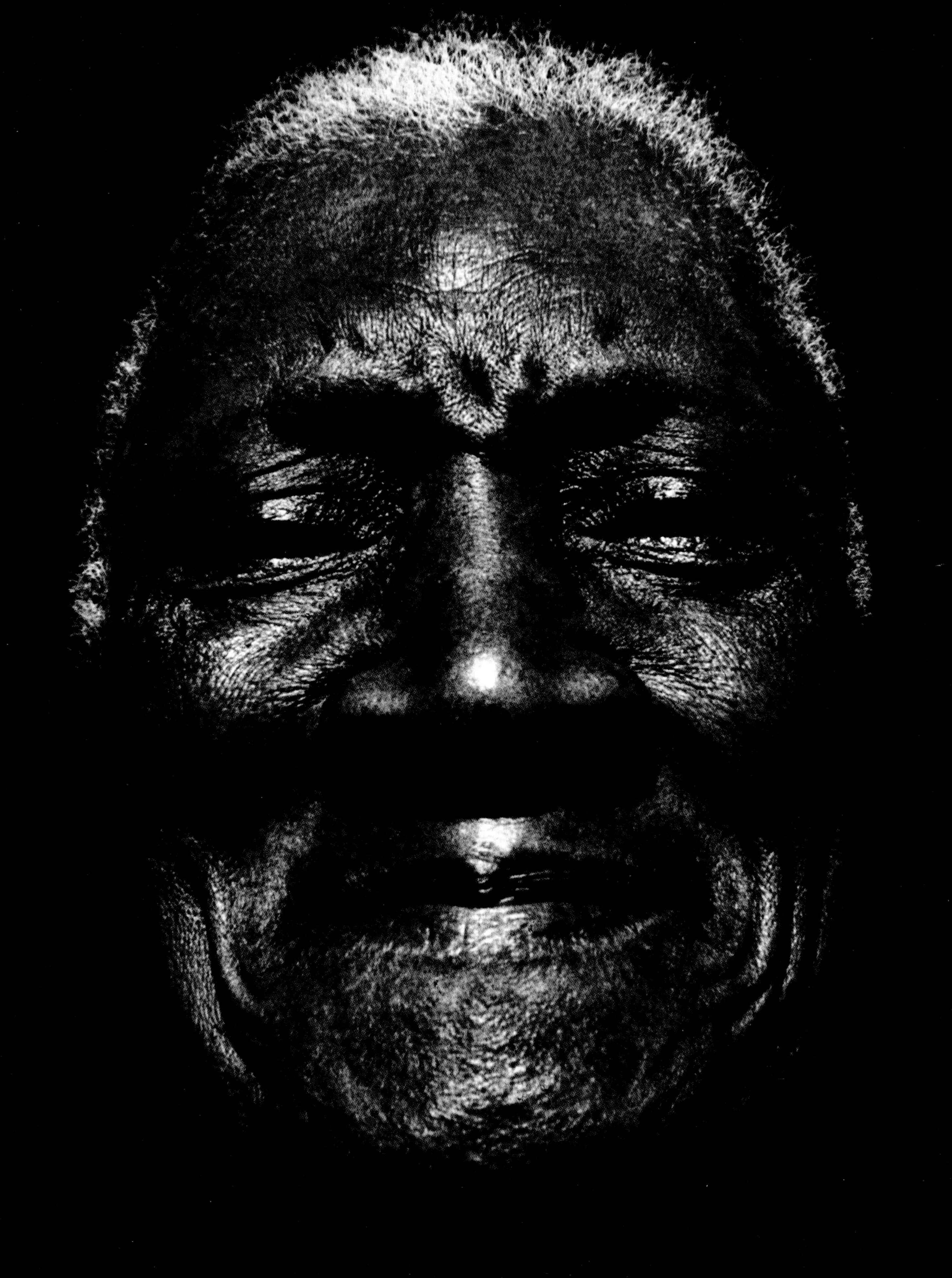

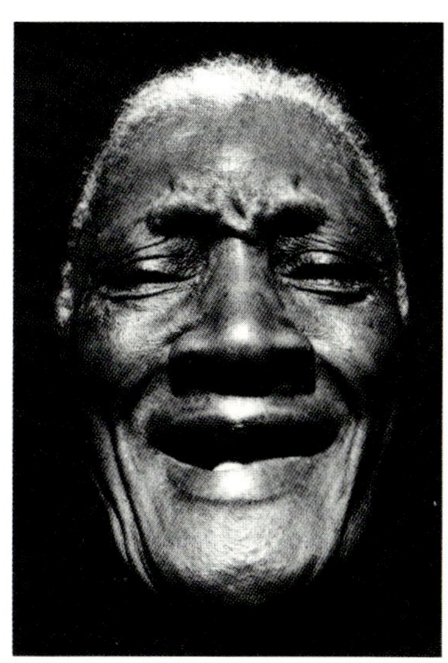

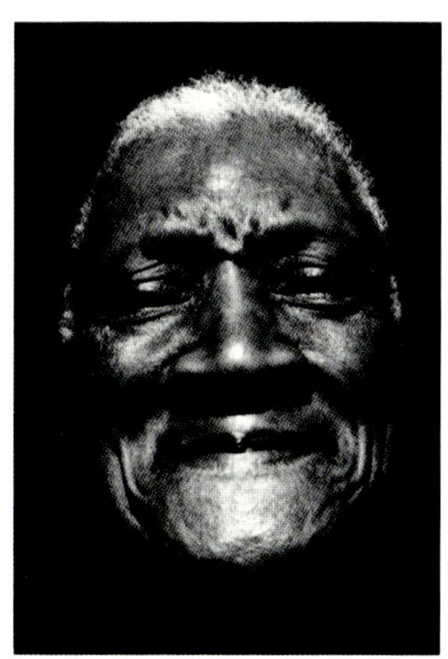

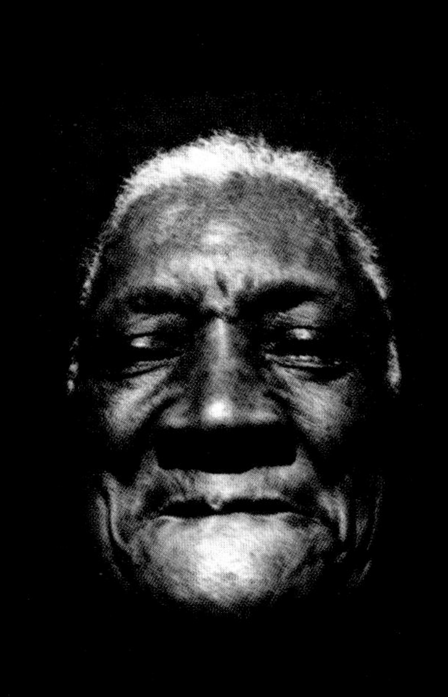

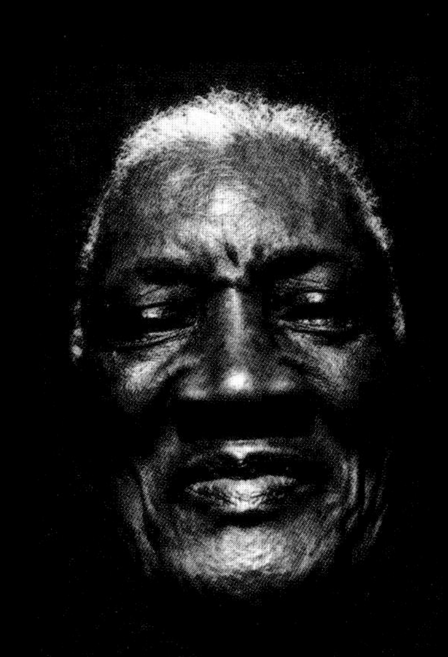

INDIAN PRINCESS

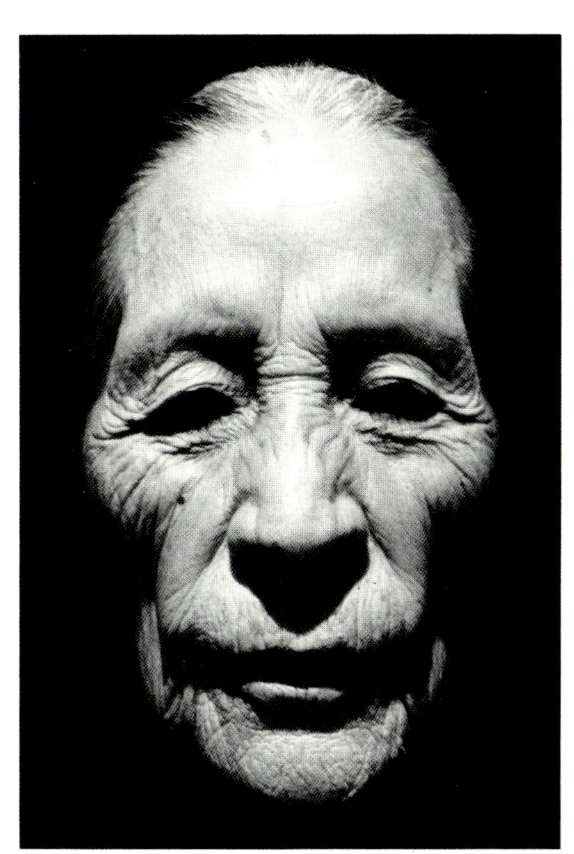

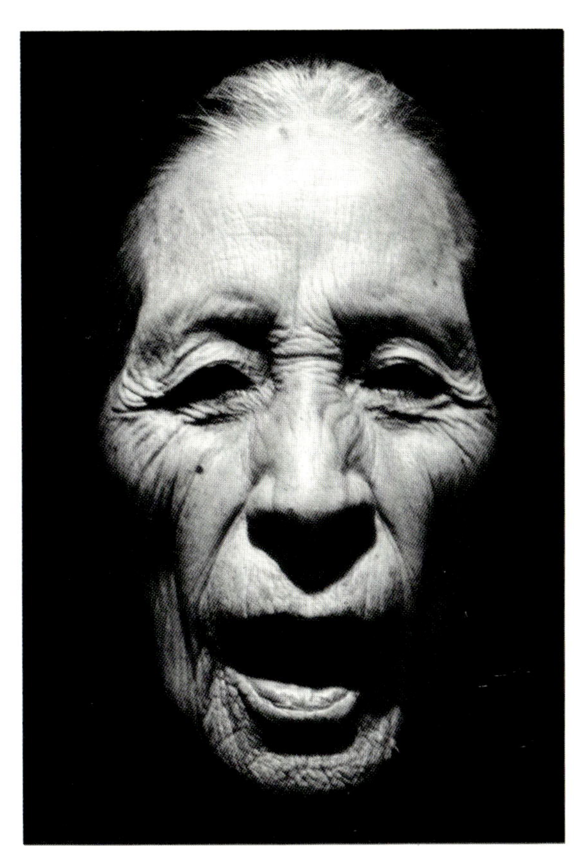

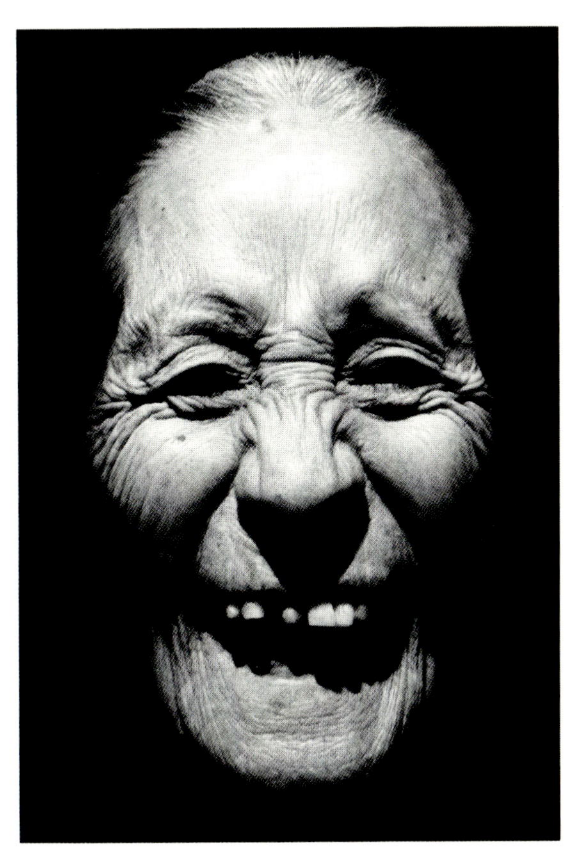

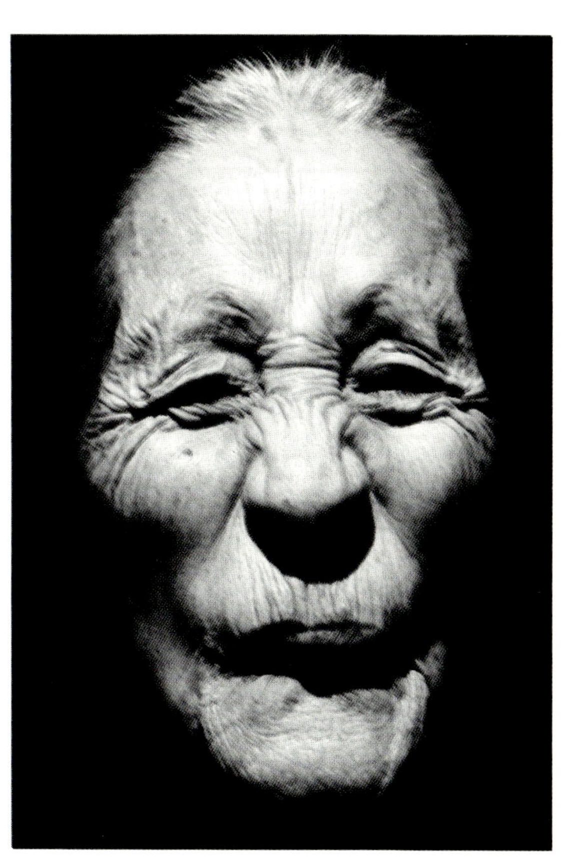

MELONIE

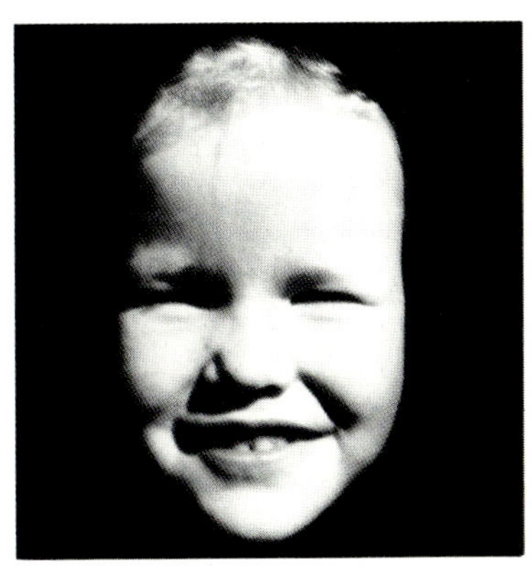

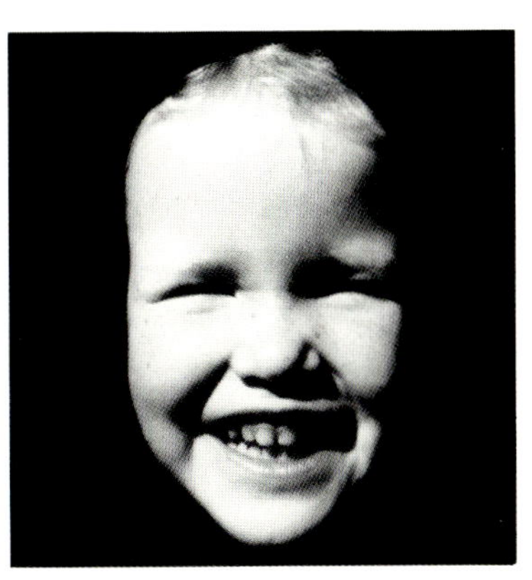

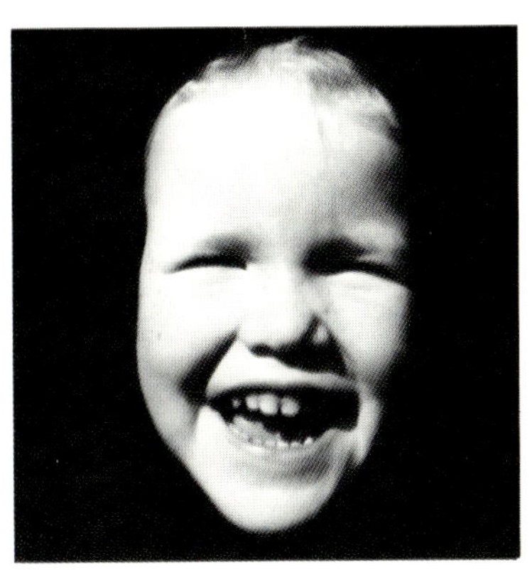

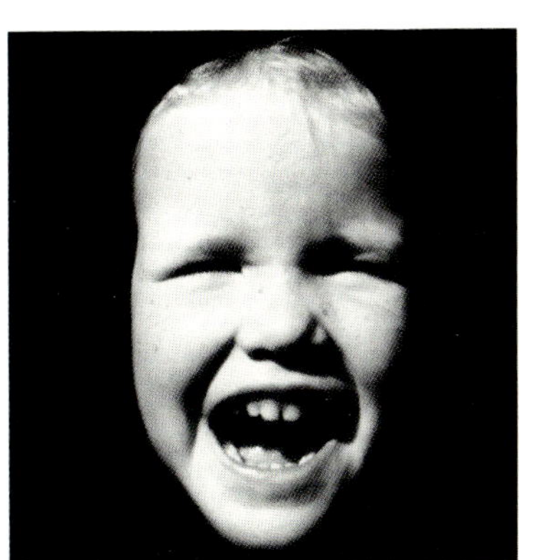

BLACK MAN

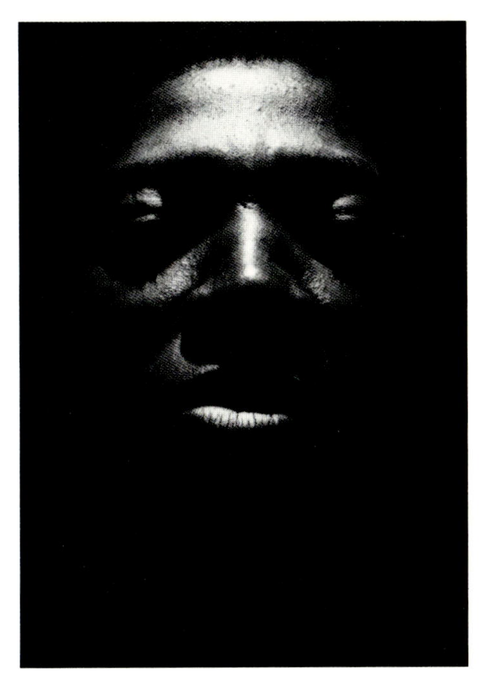 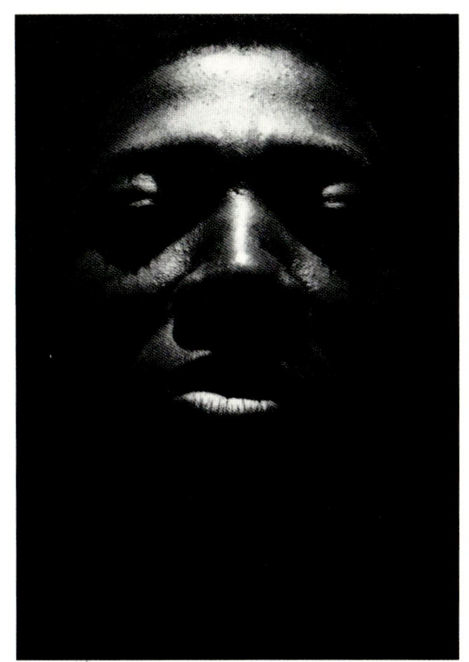

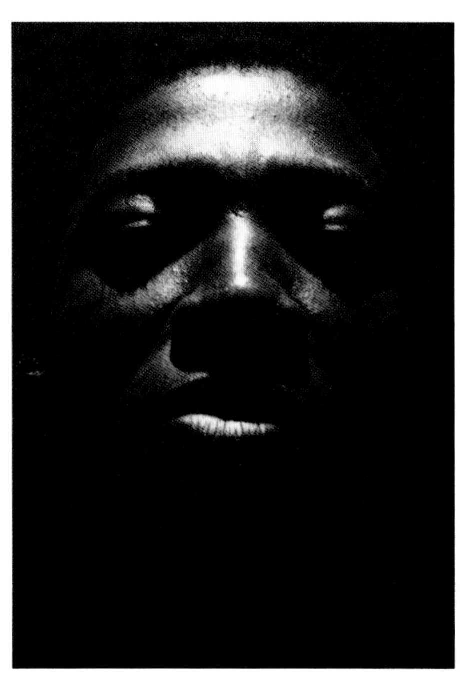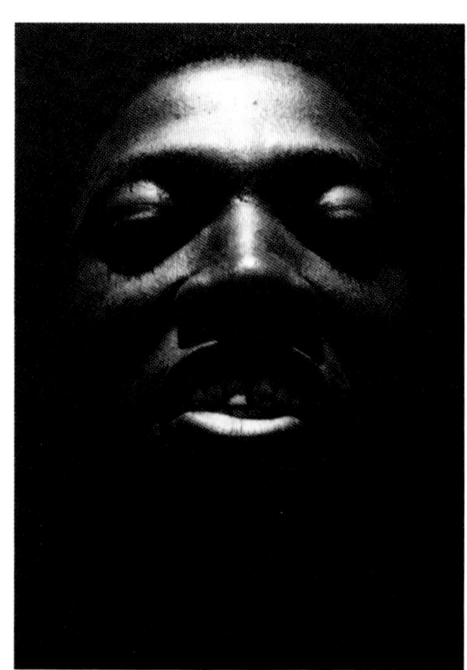

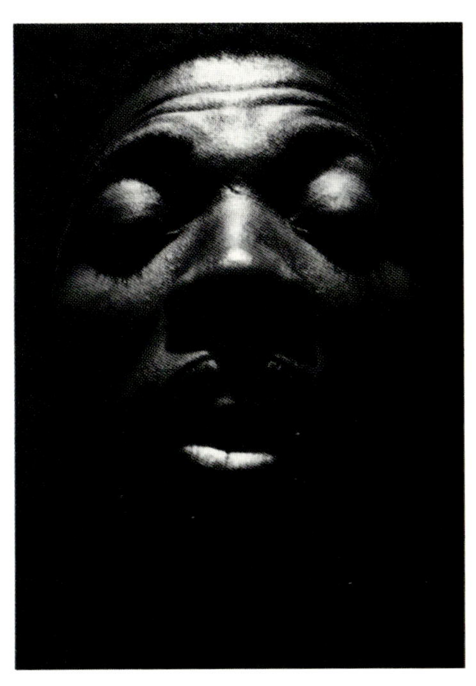 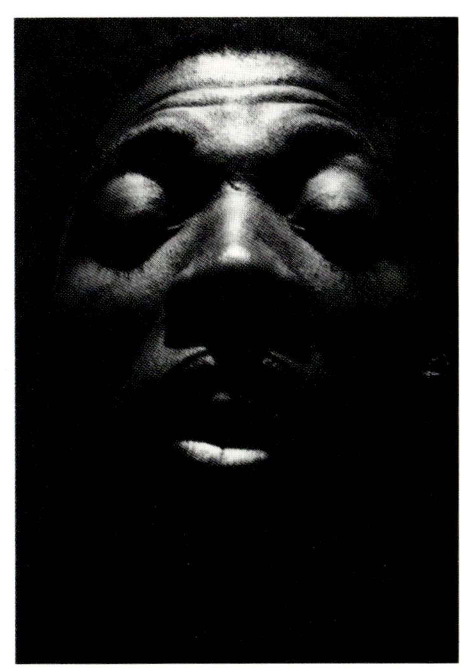

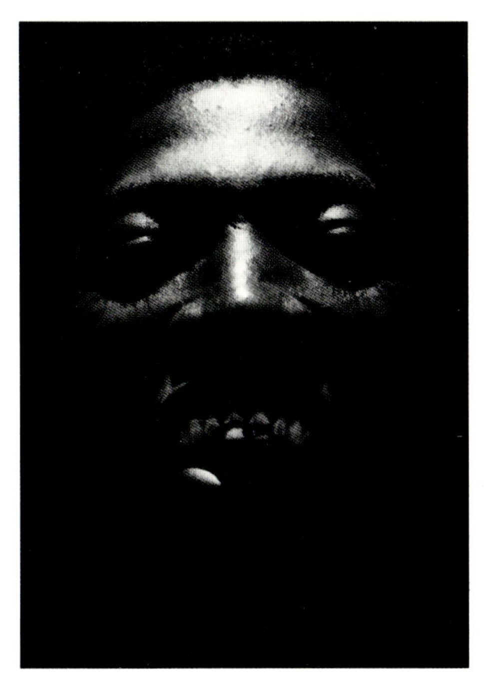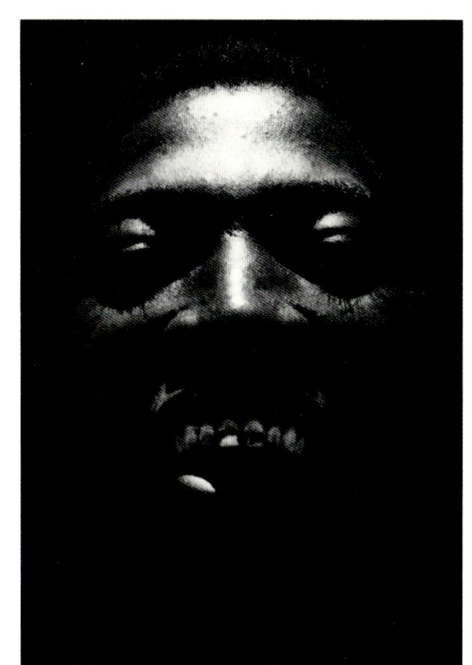

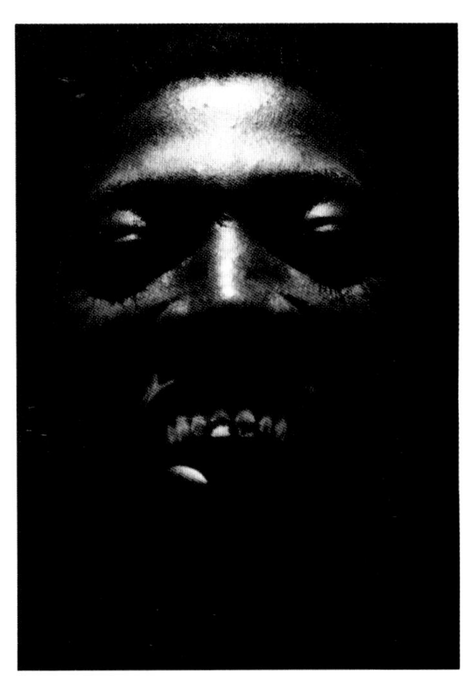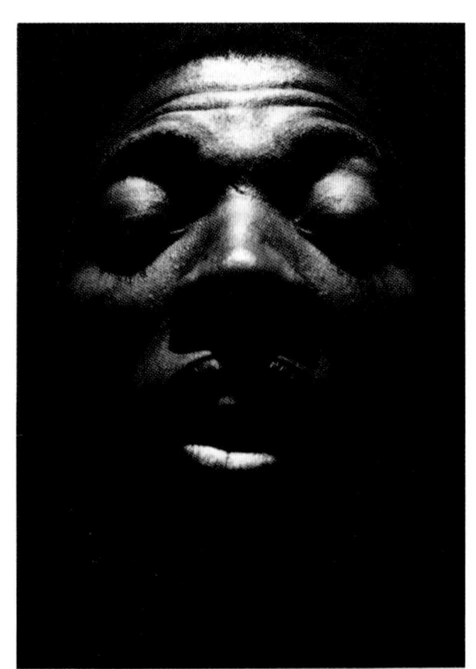

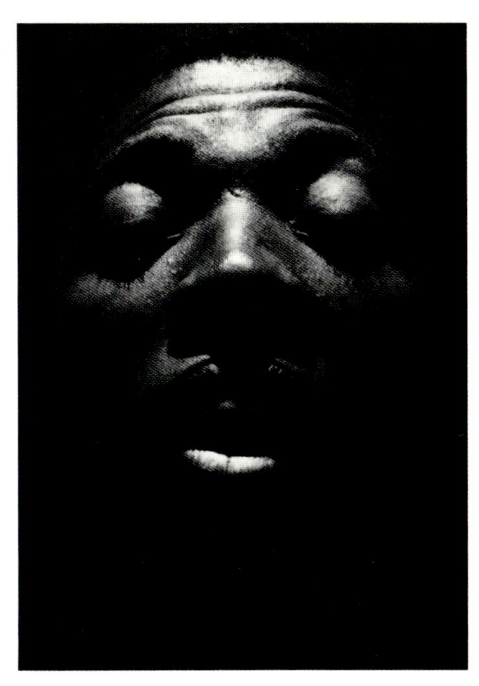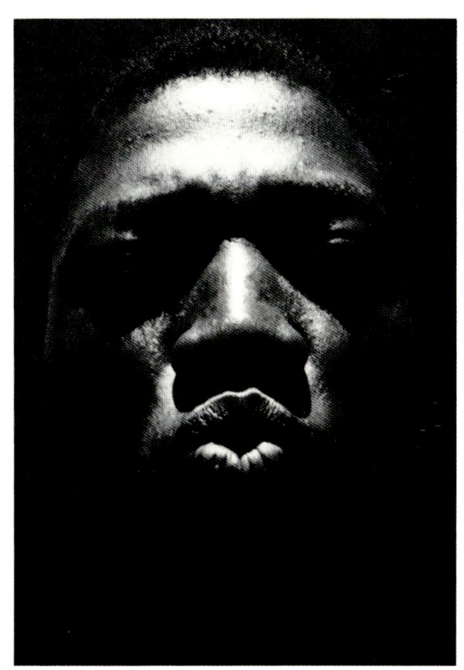

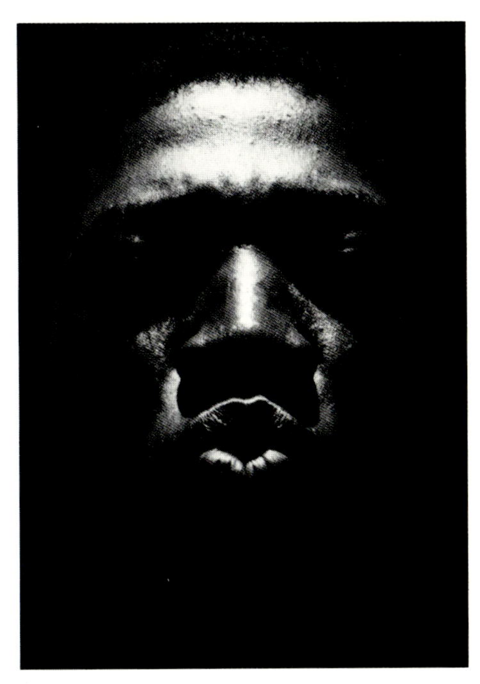 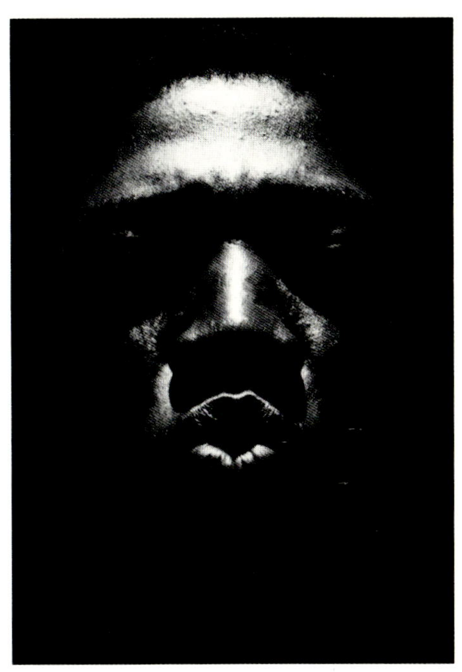

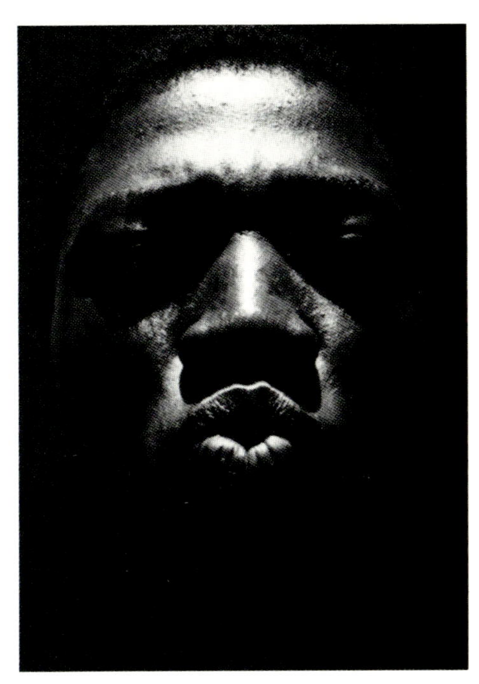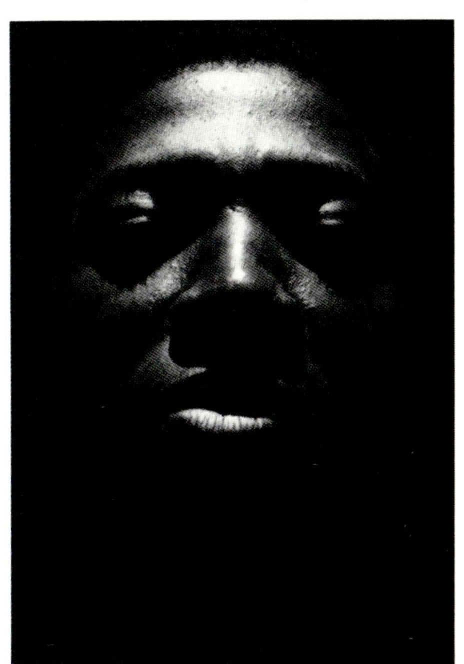

ACE

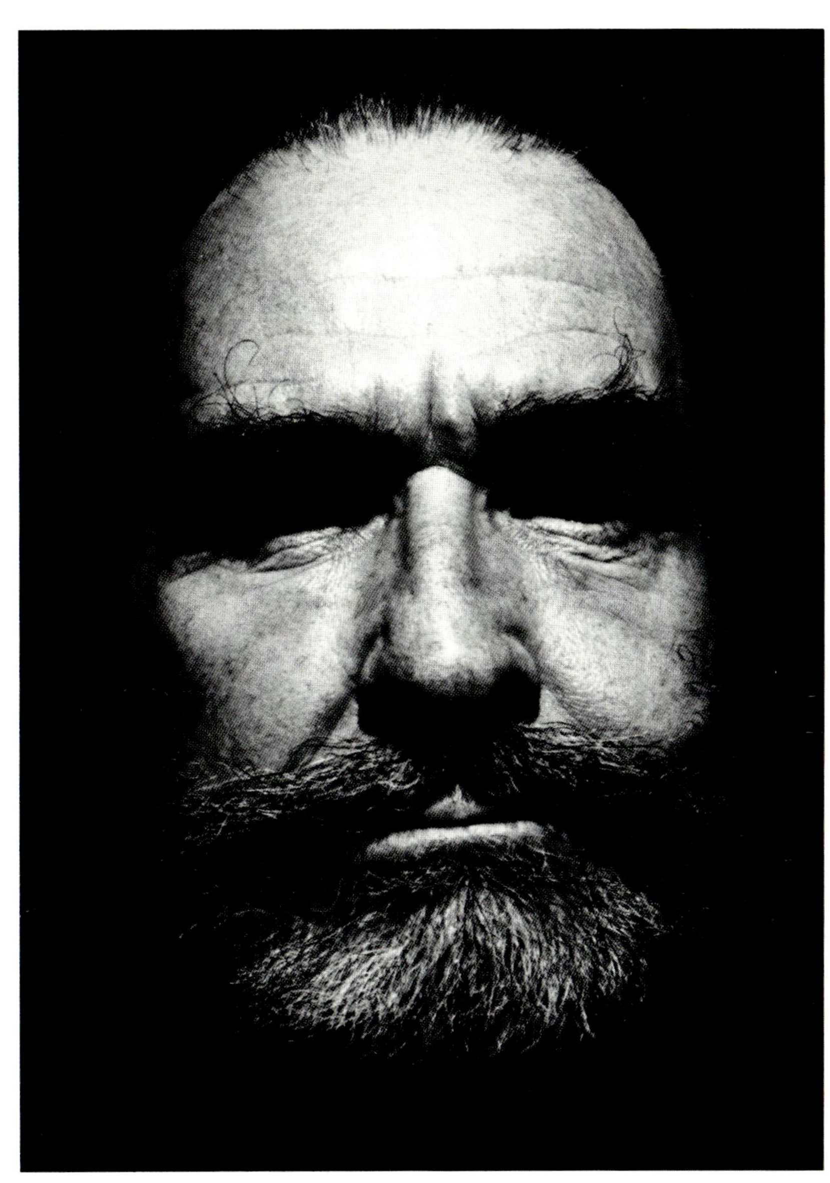

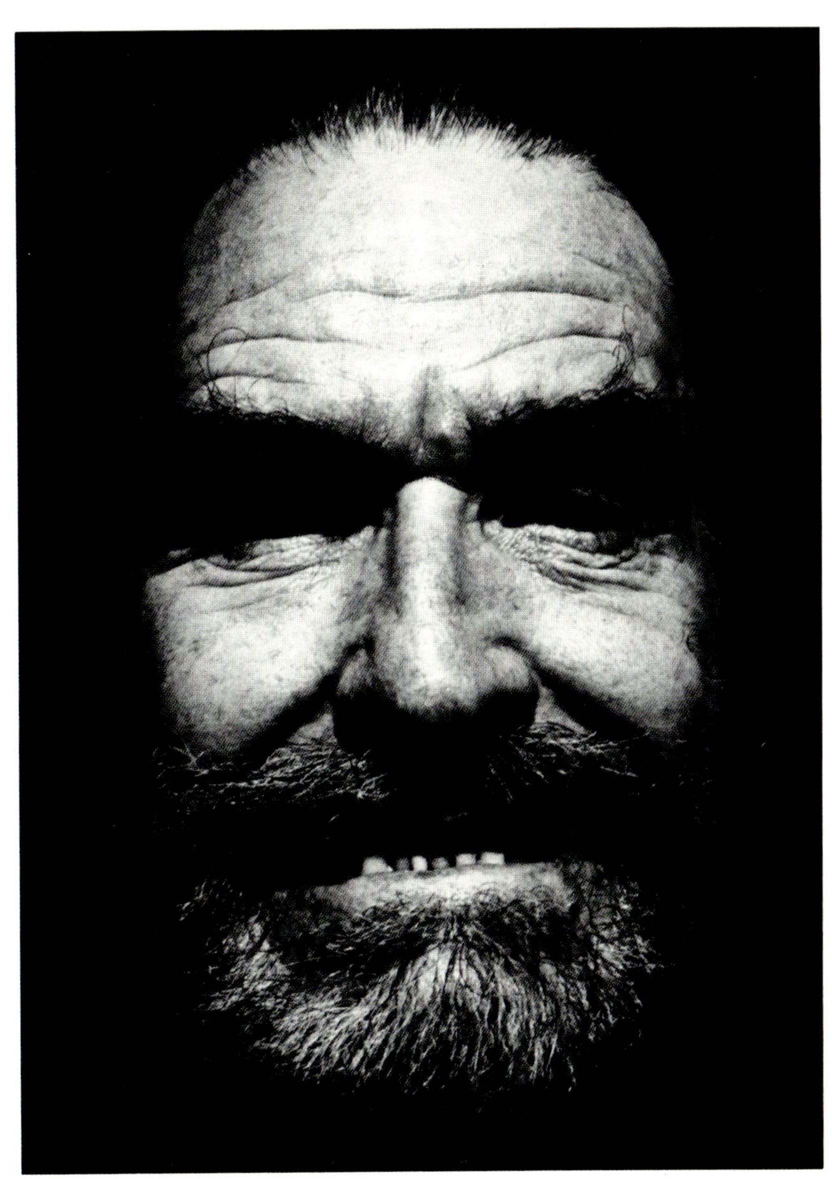

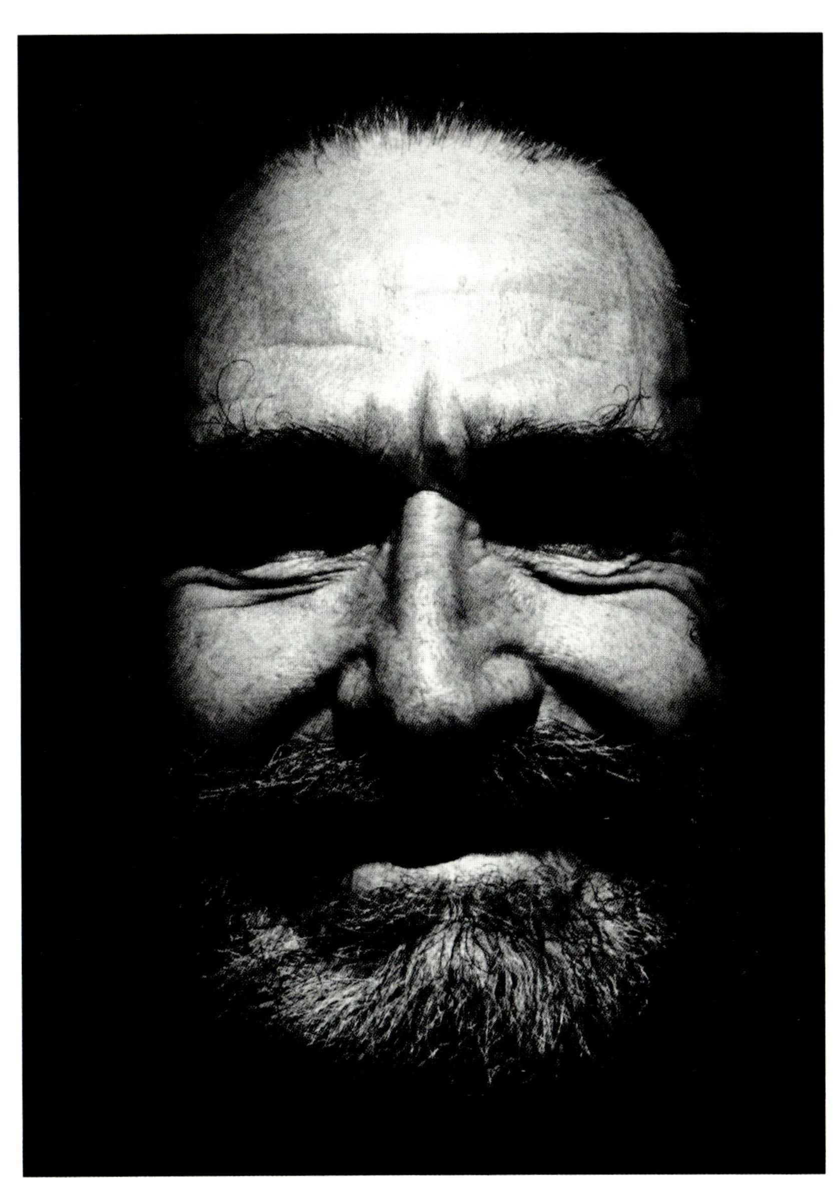

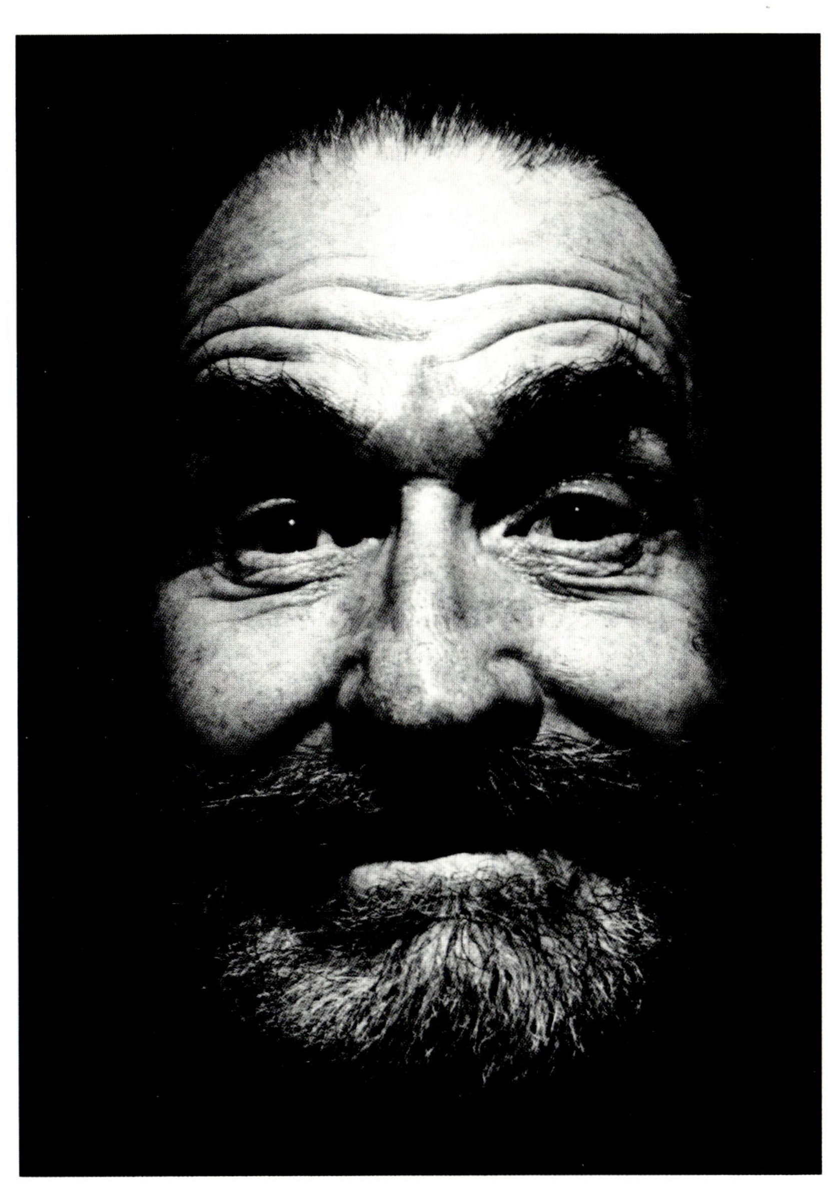

PHU

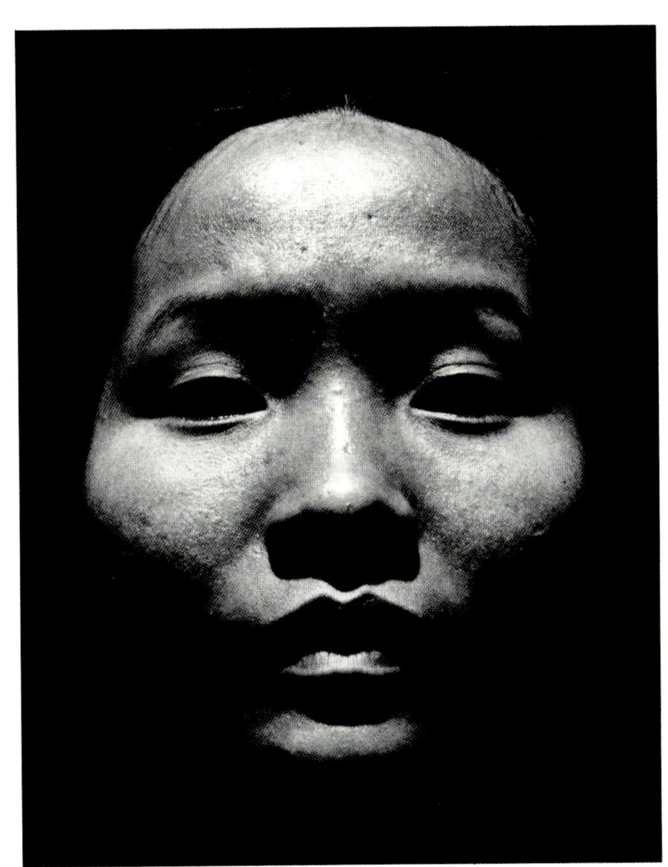

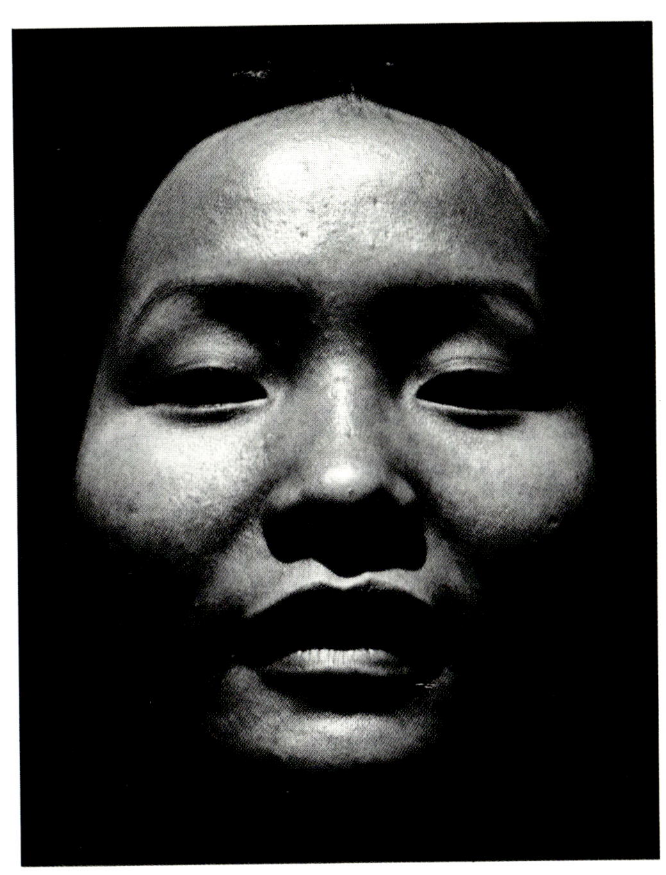

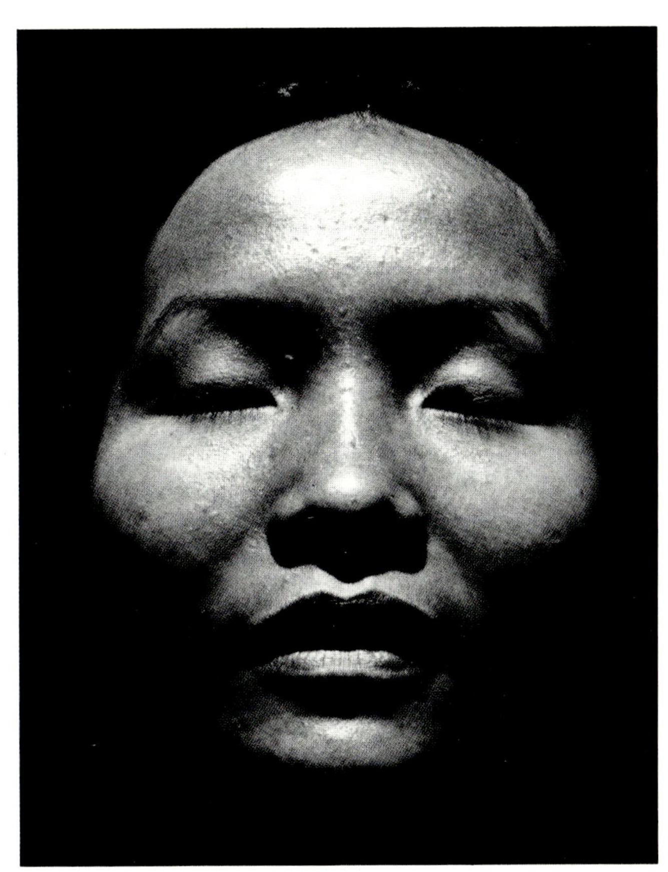

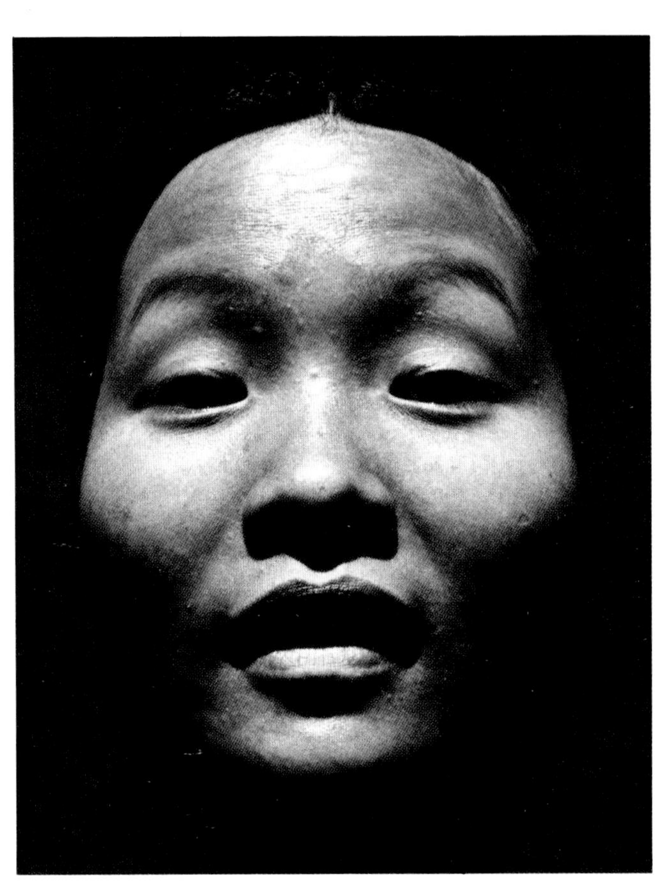

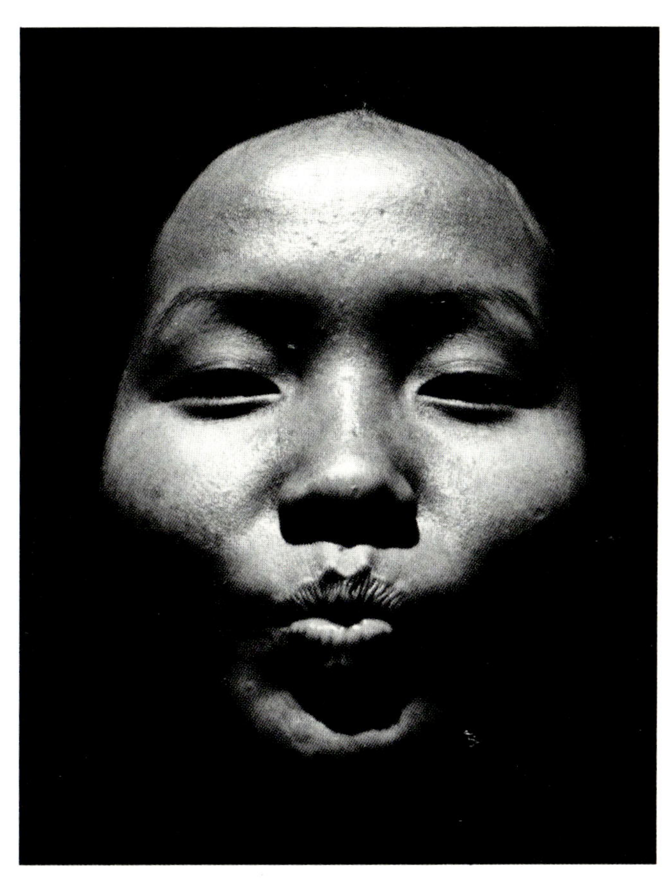

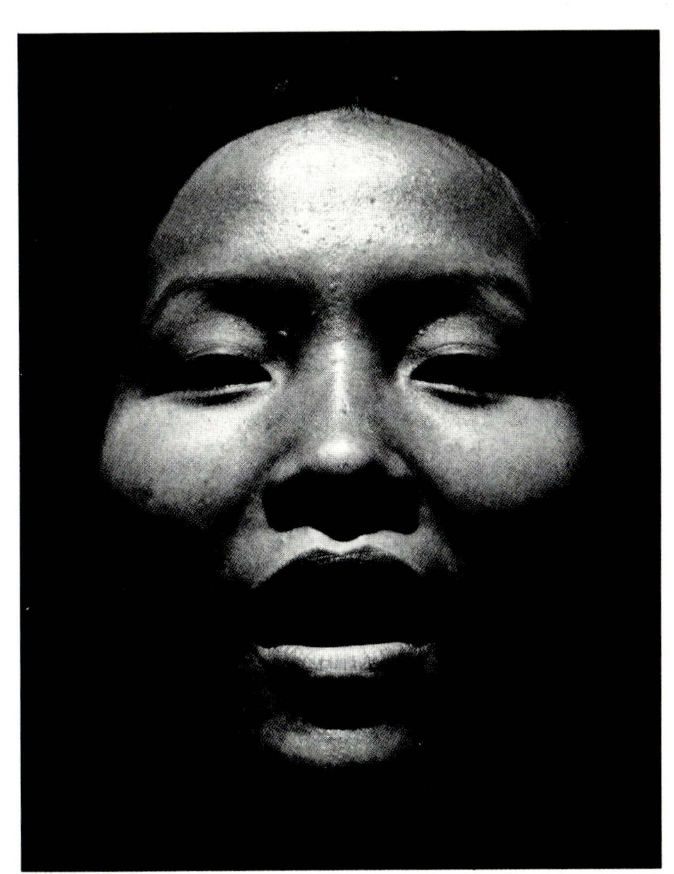

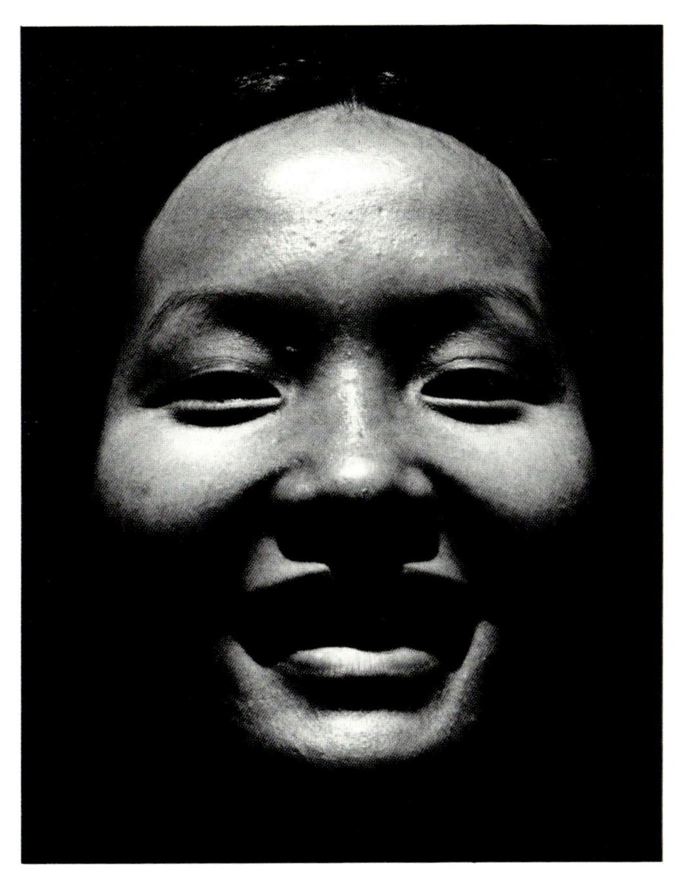

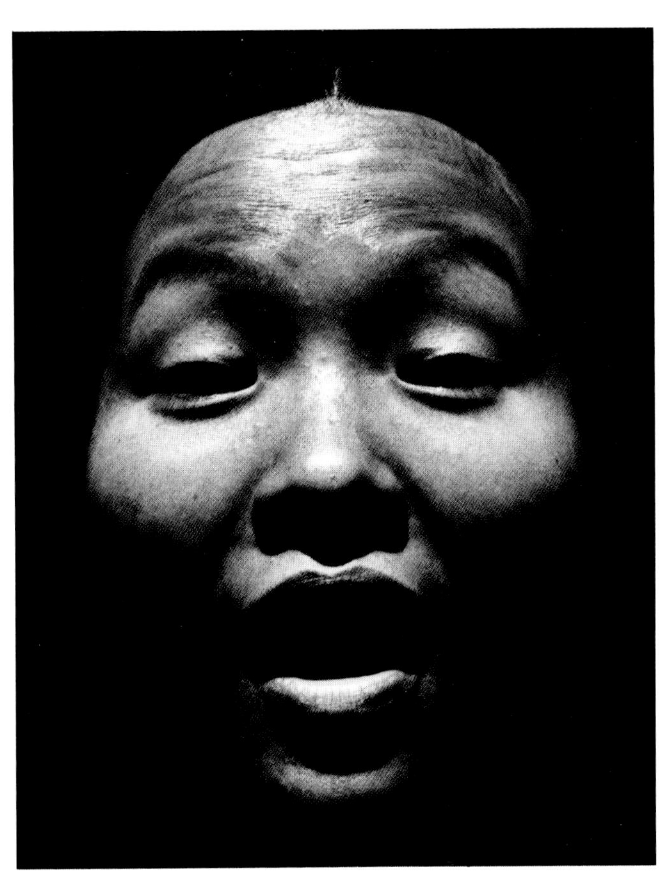

EURA

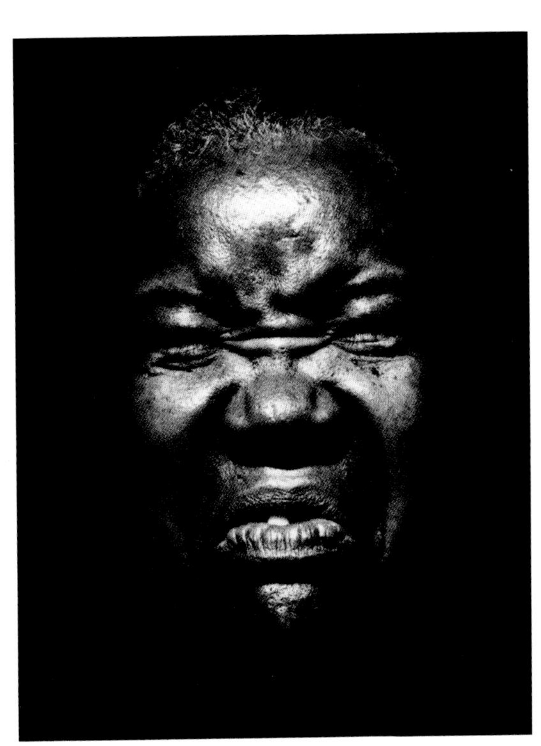

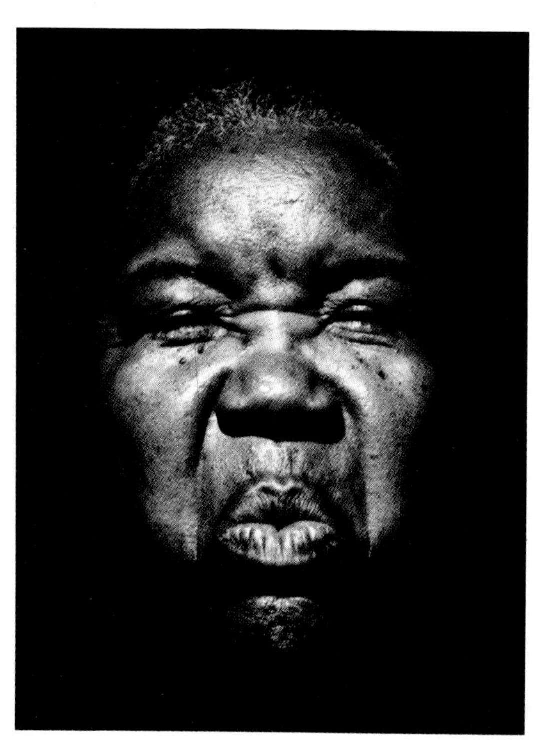

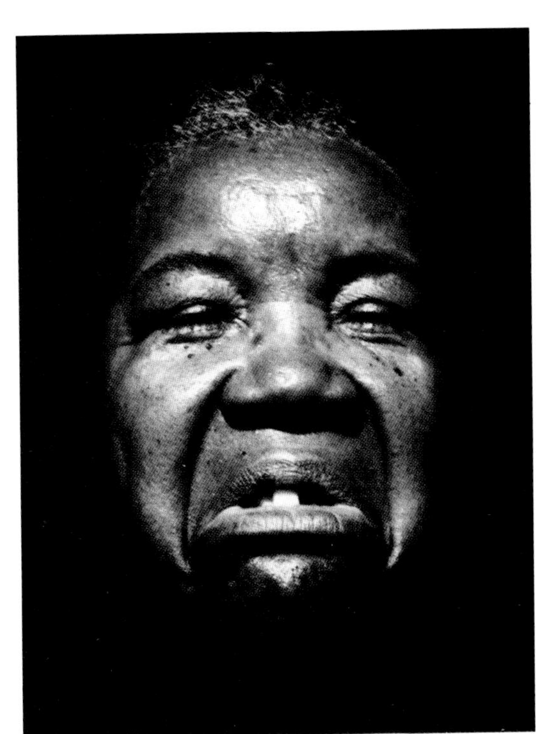

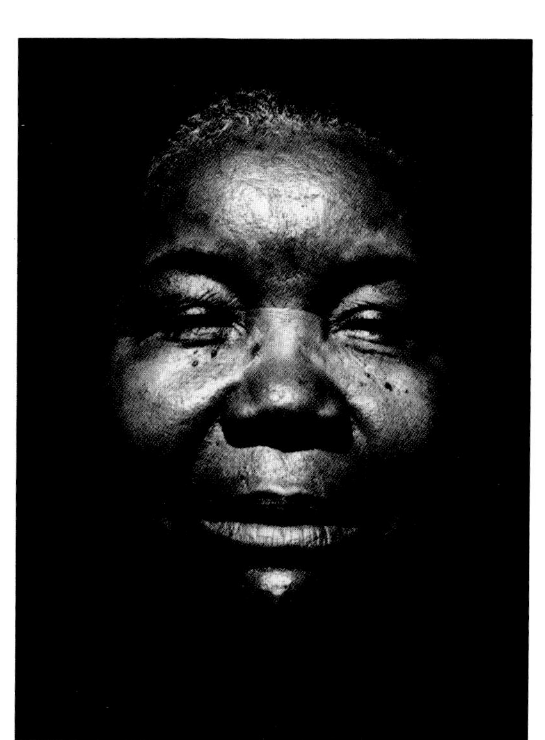

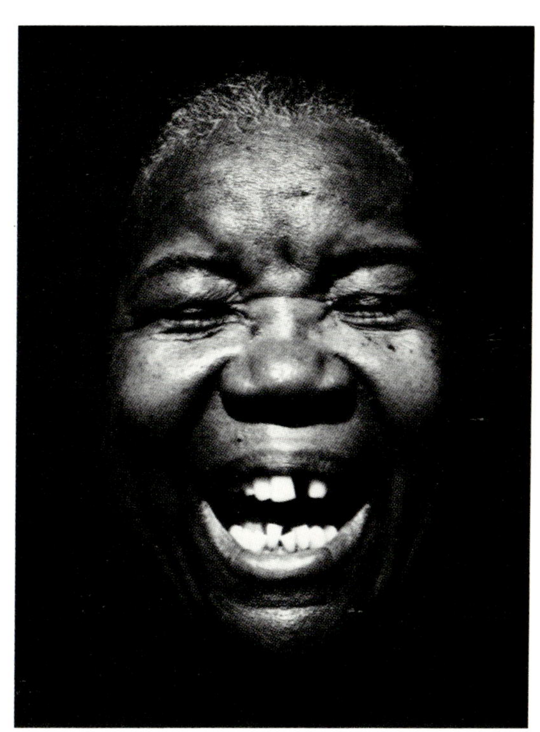

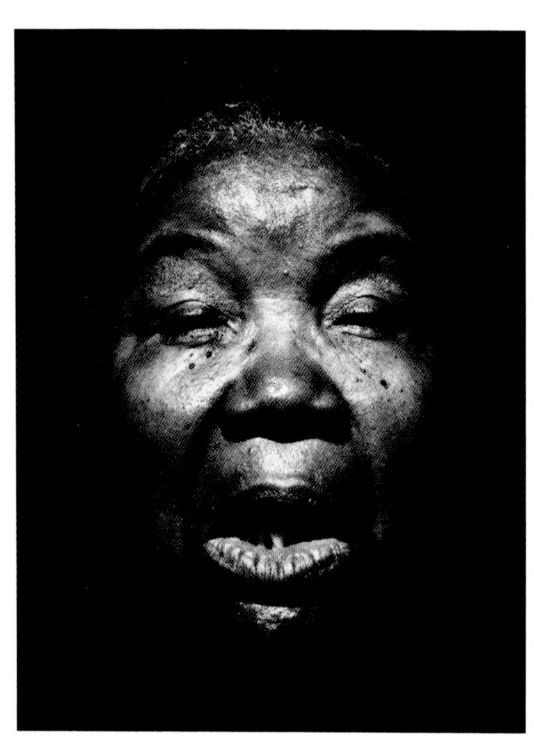

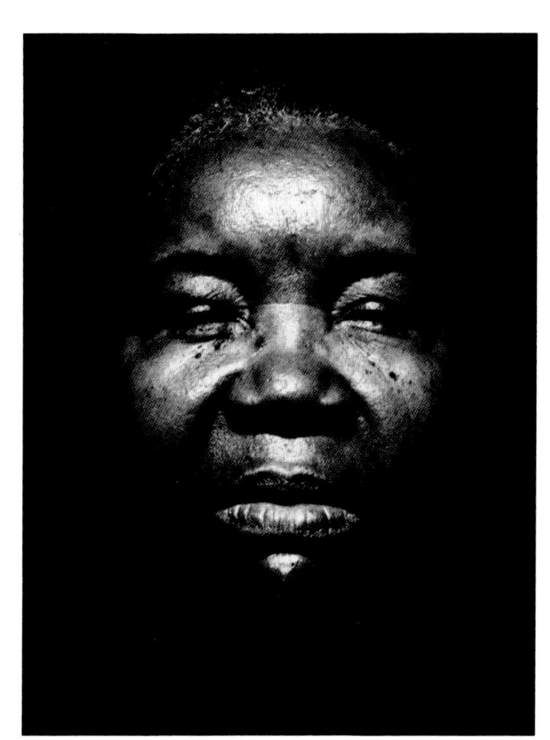

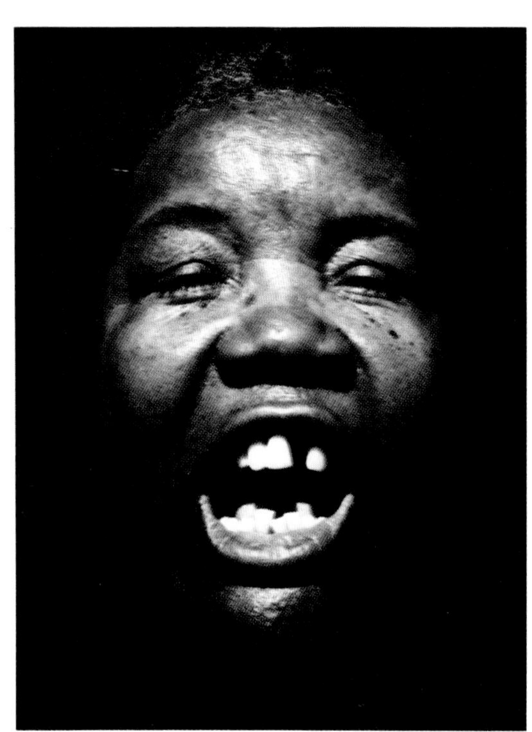

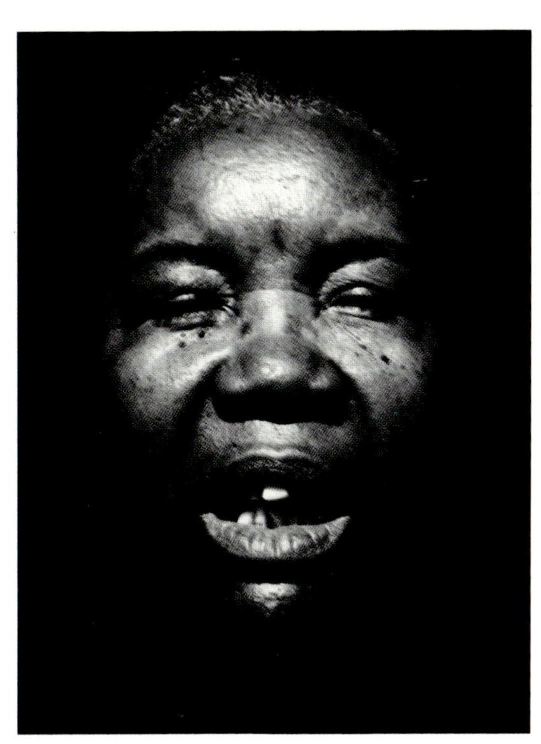

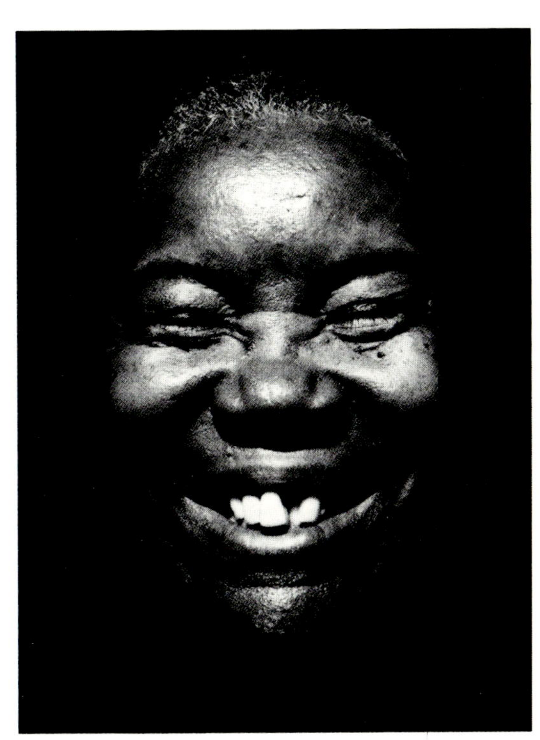

NICHOLAS

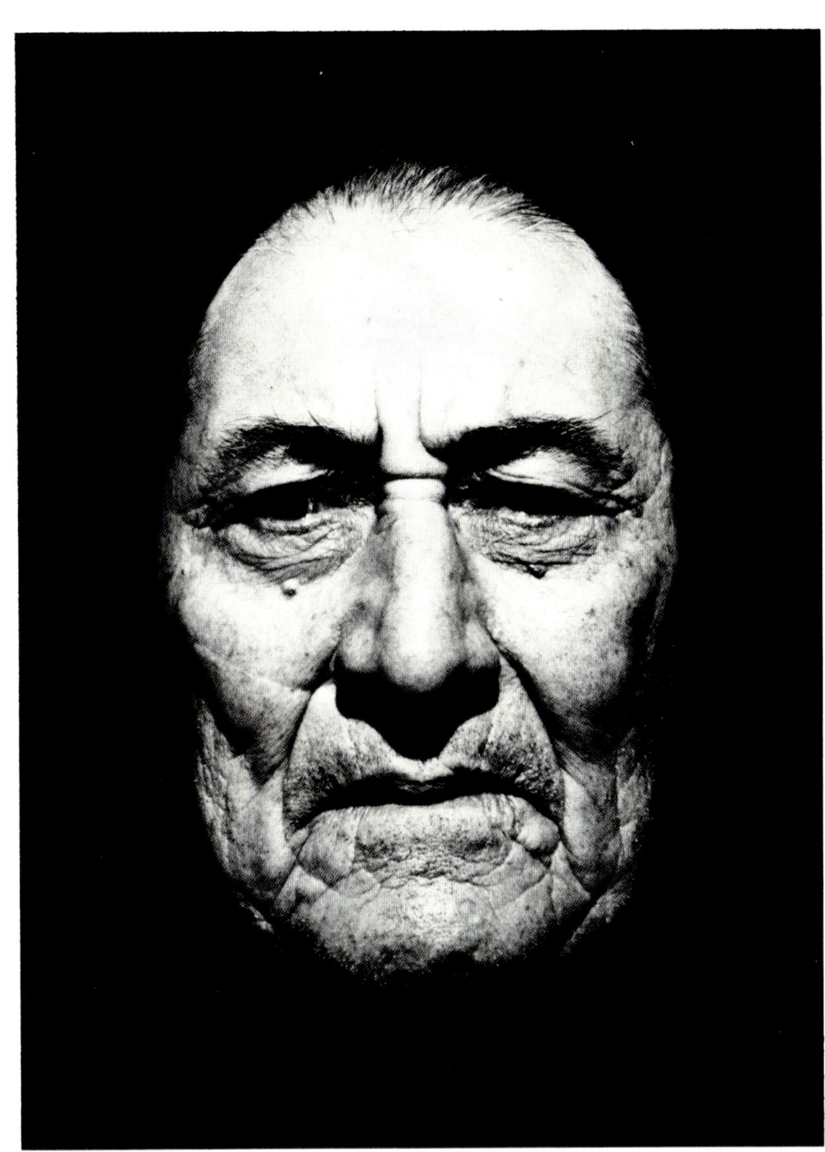

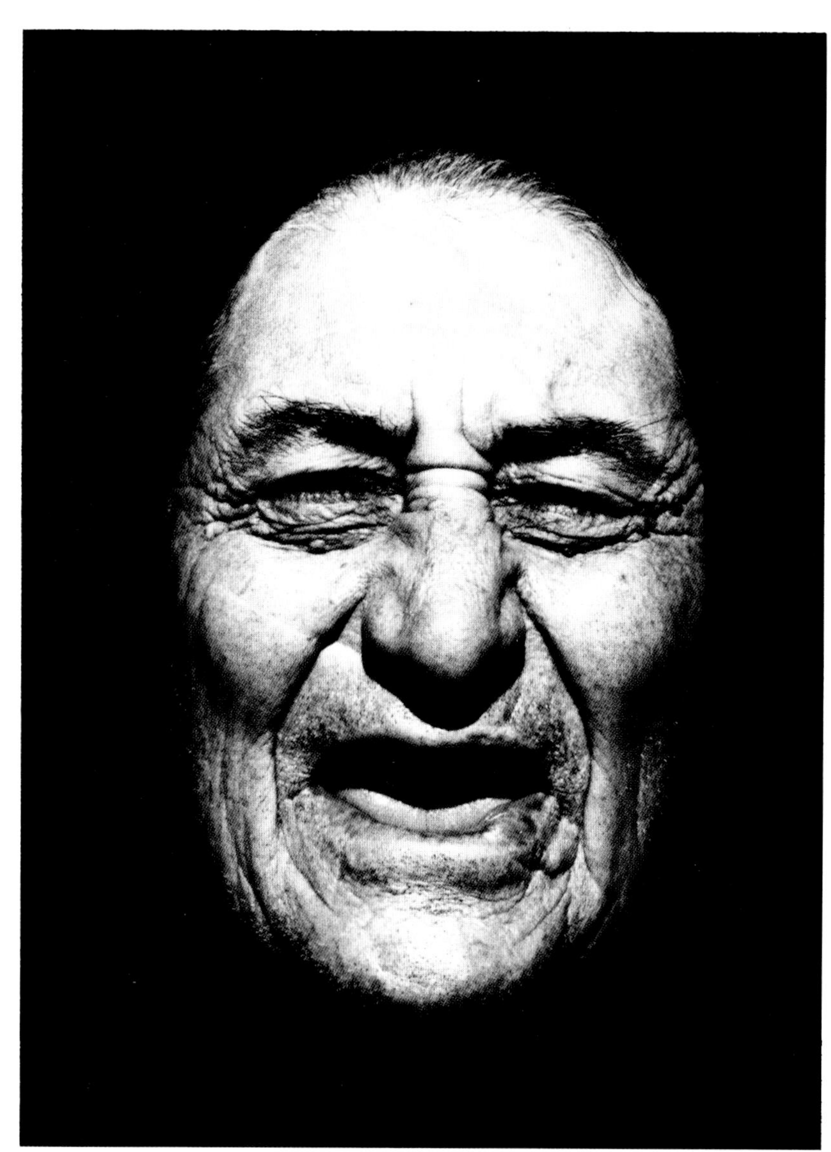

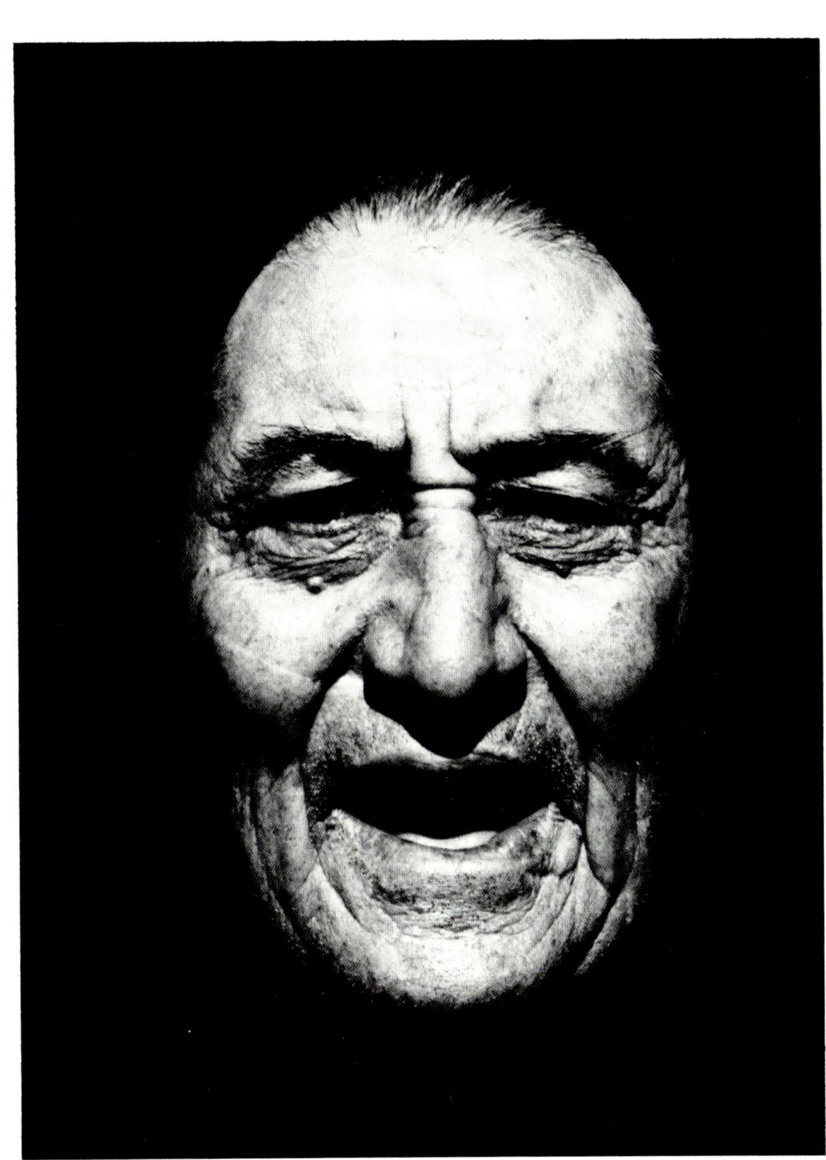

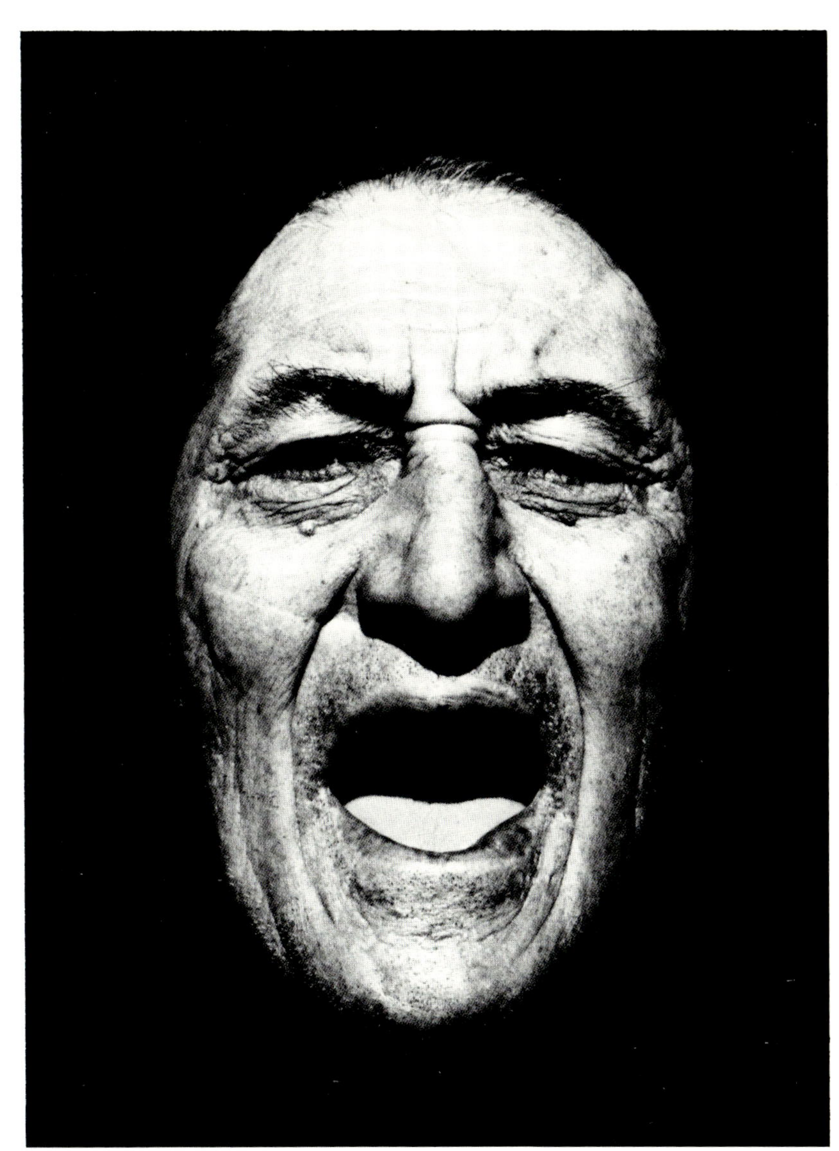

DONNA

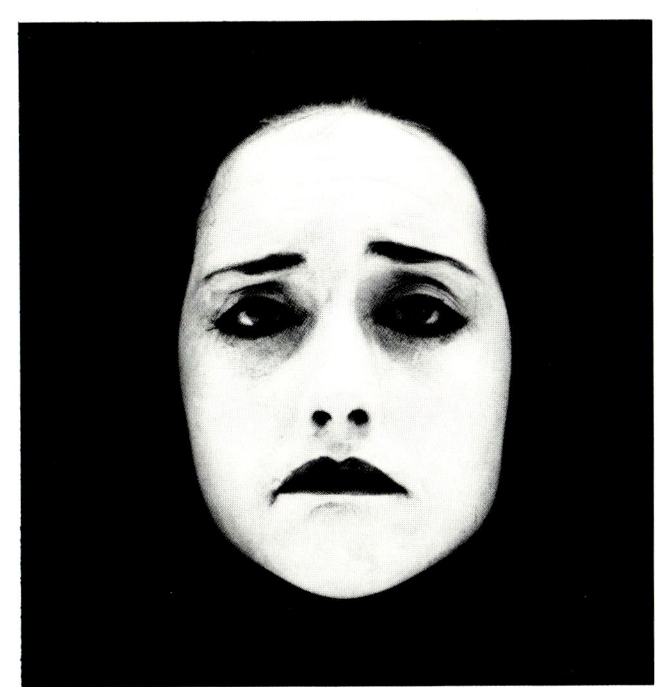

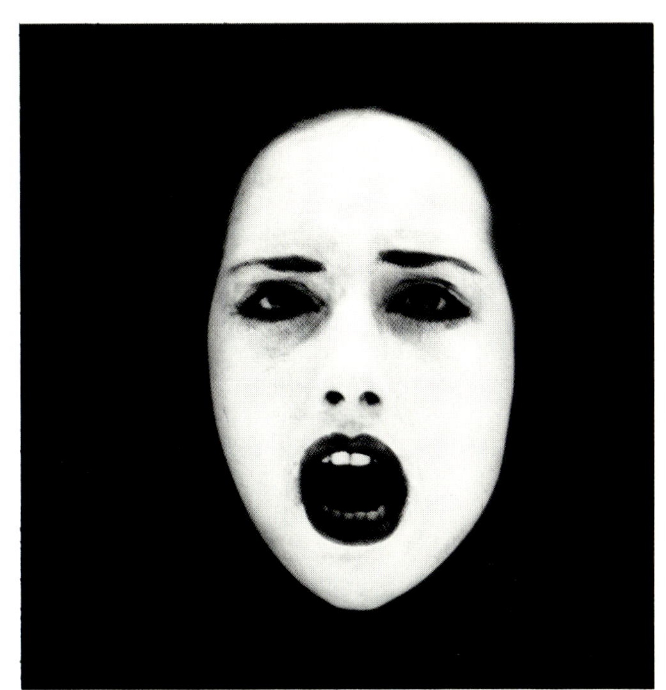

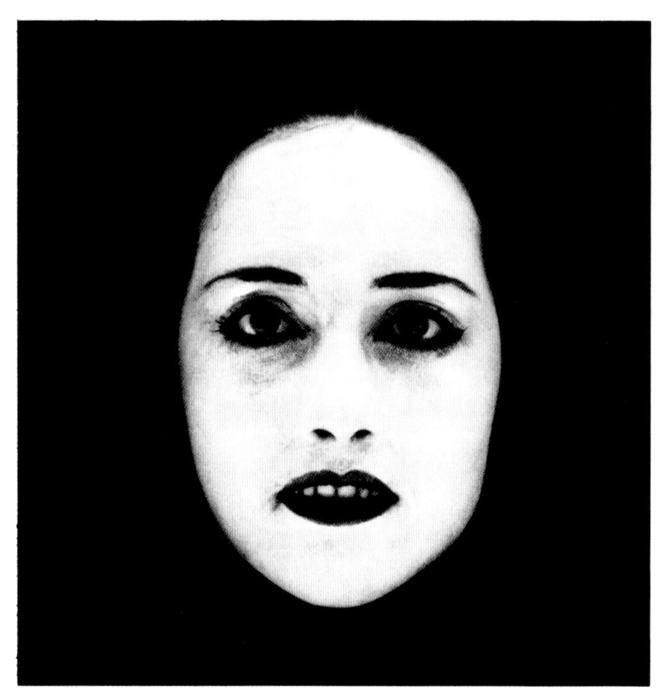

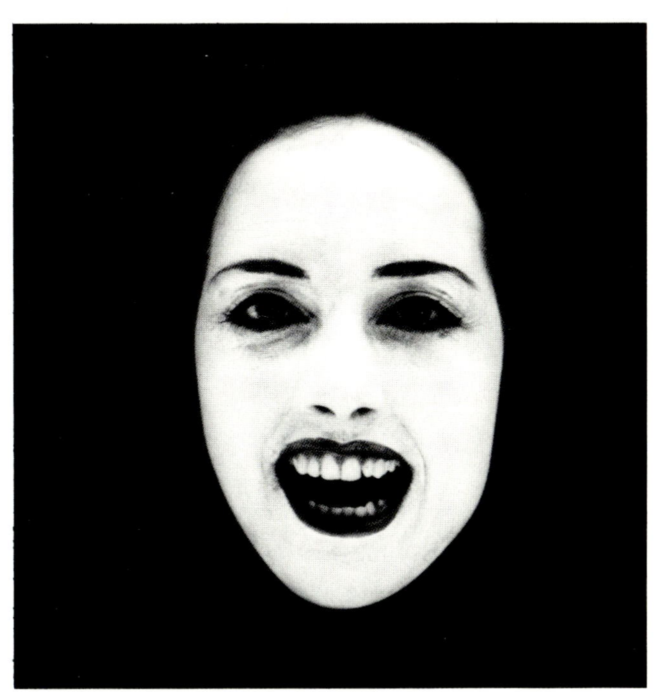

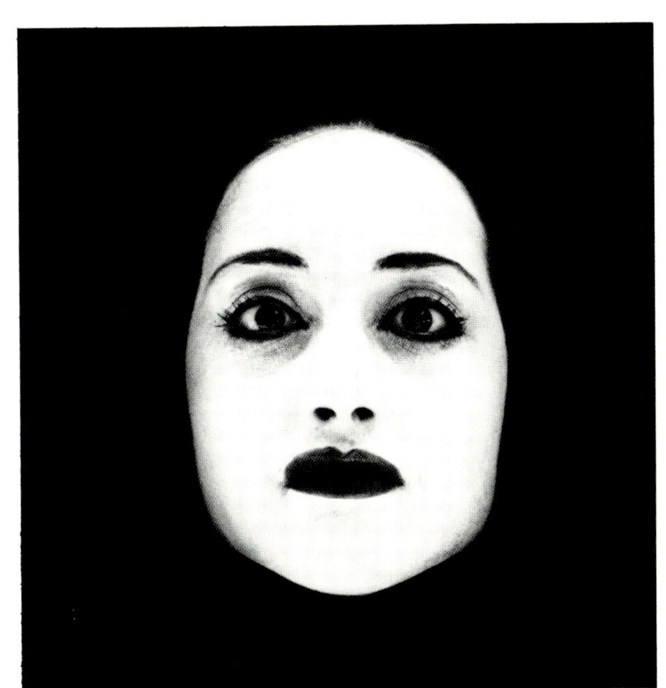

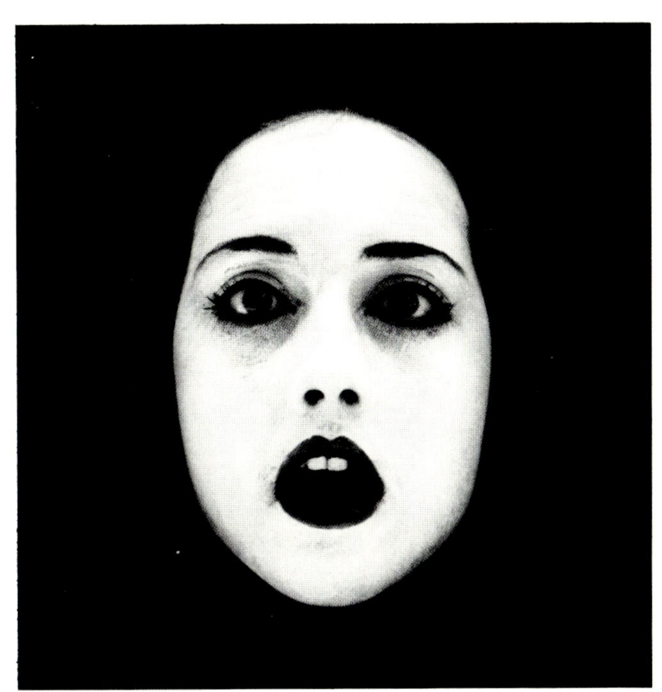

CYNTHIA

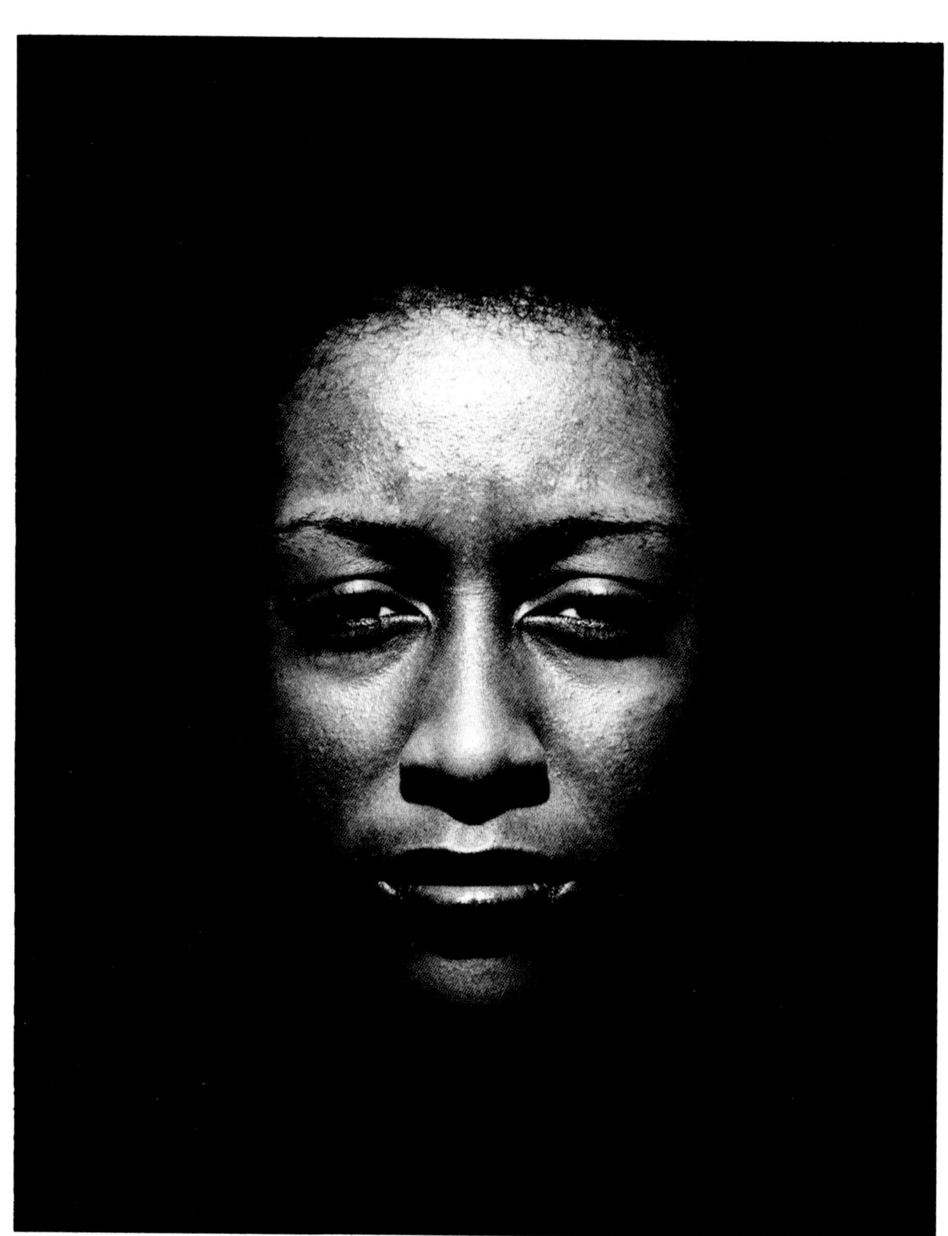

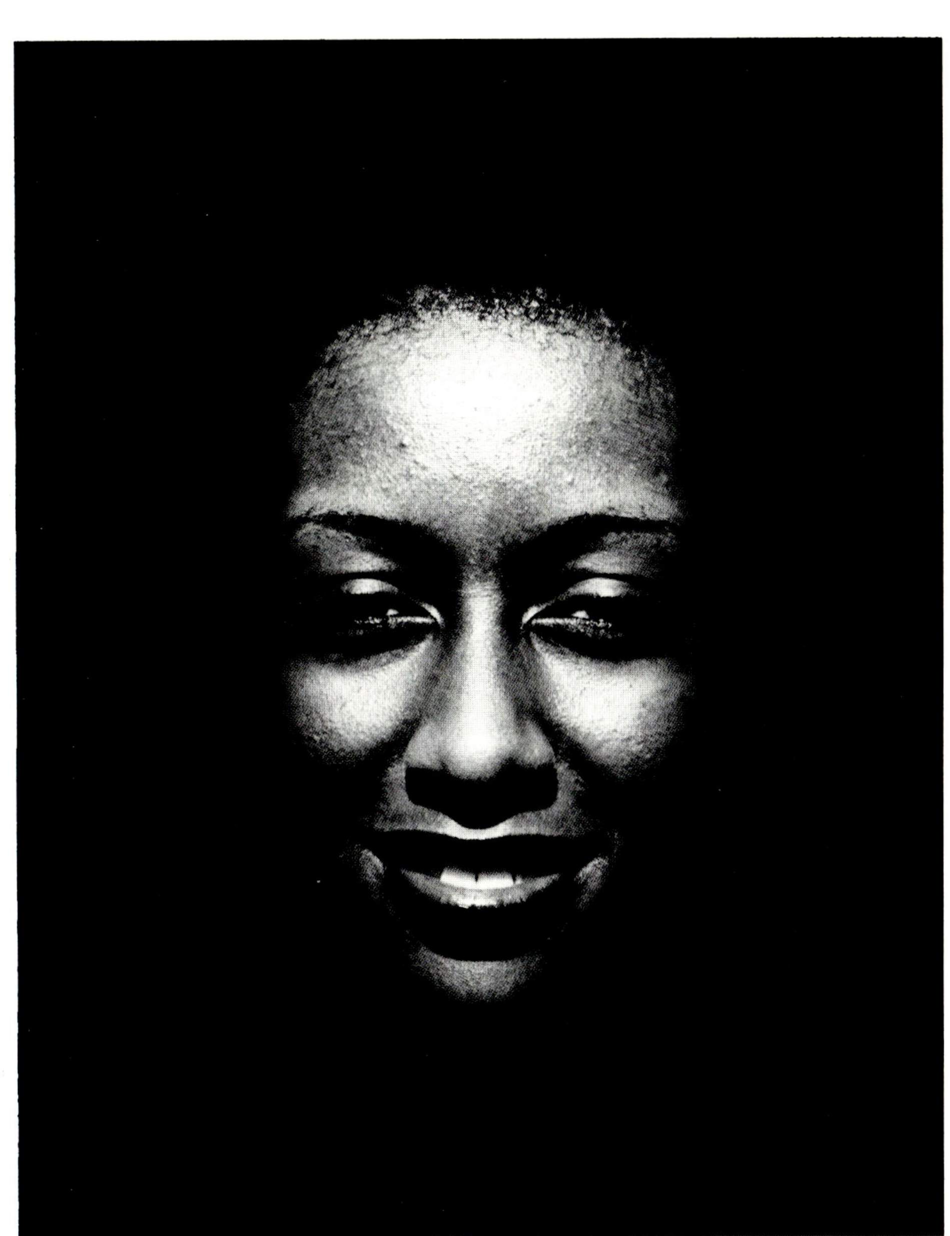

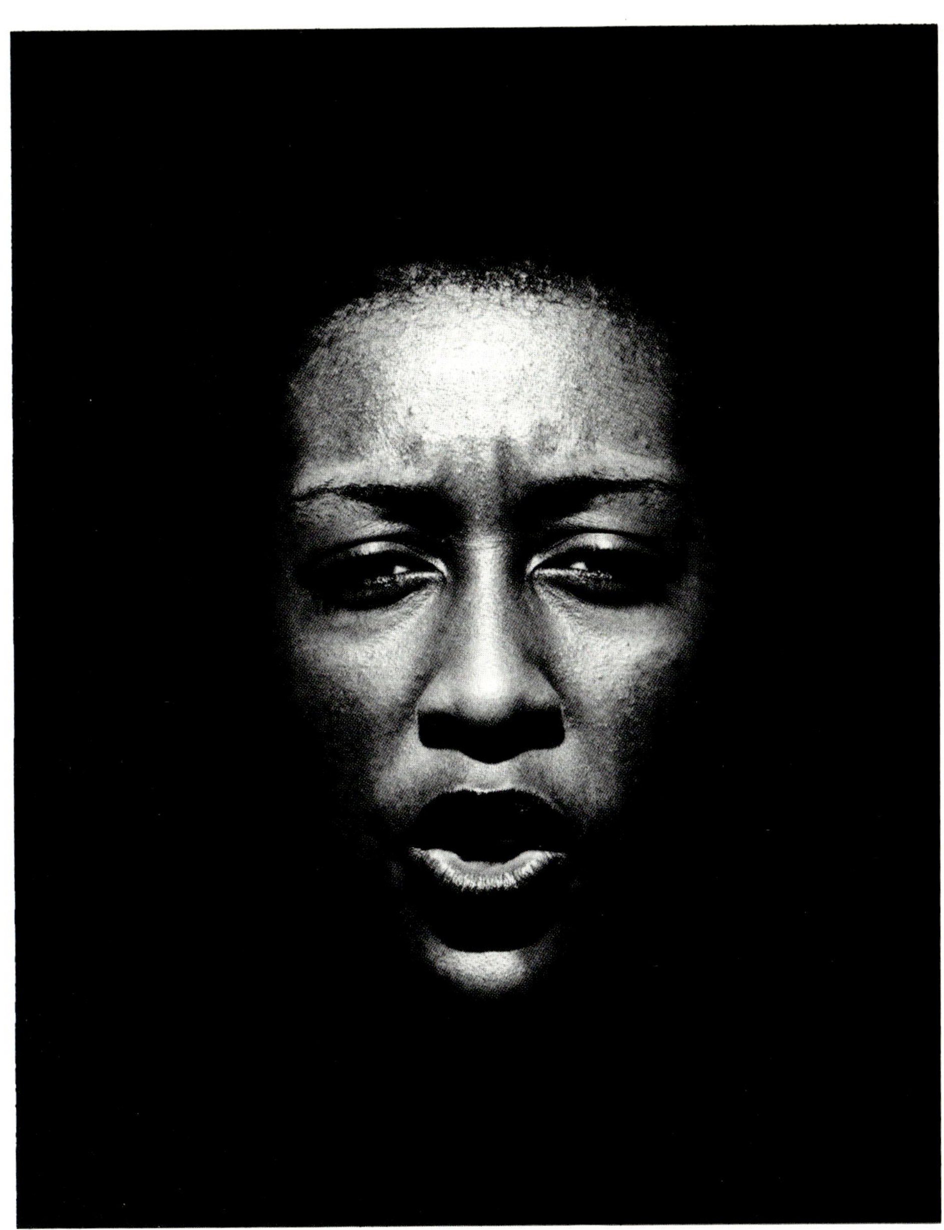

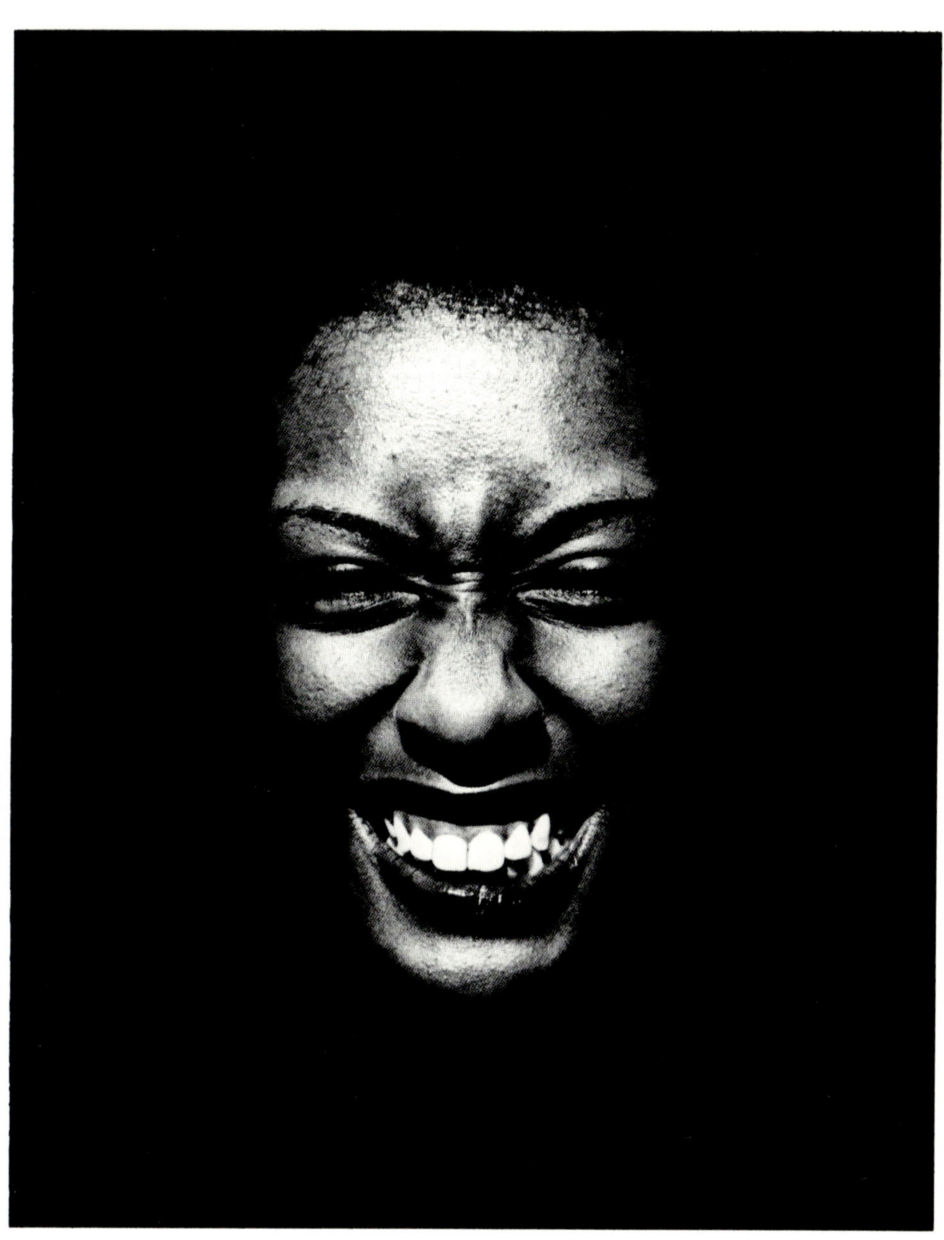

MEXICAN LADY

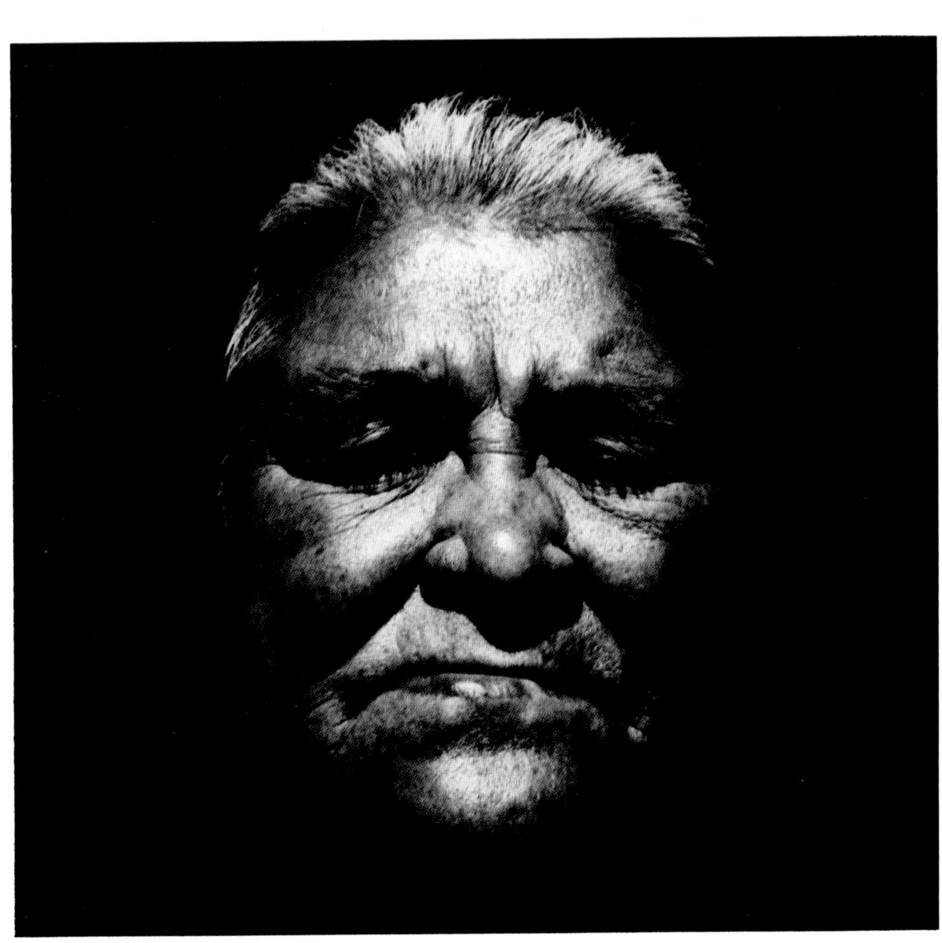

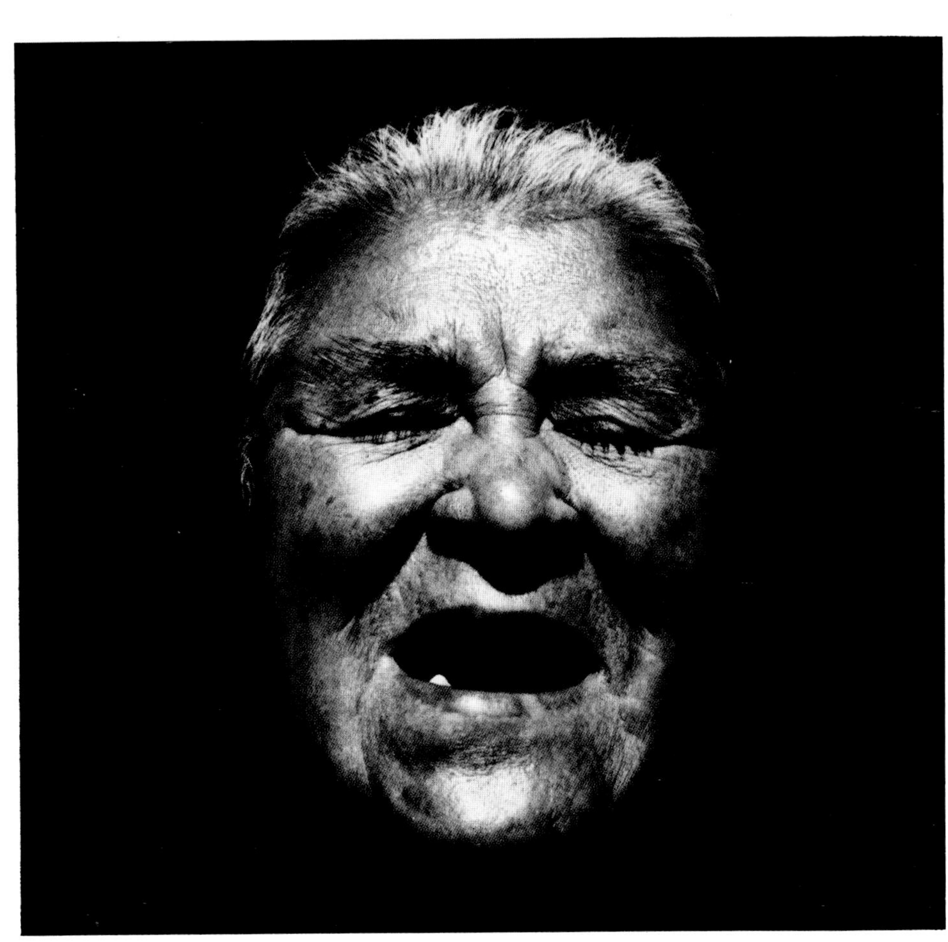

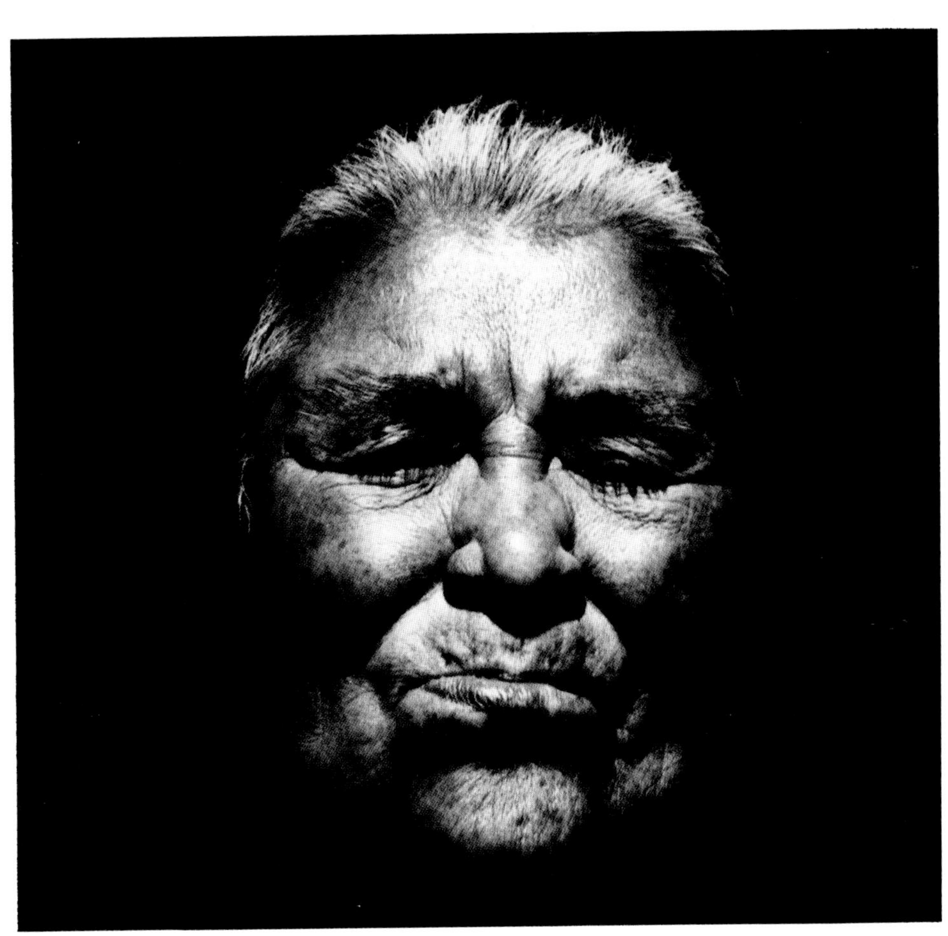

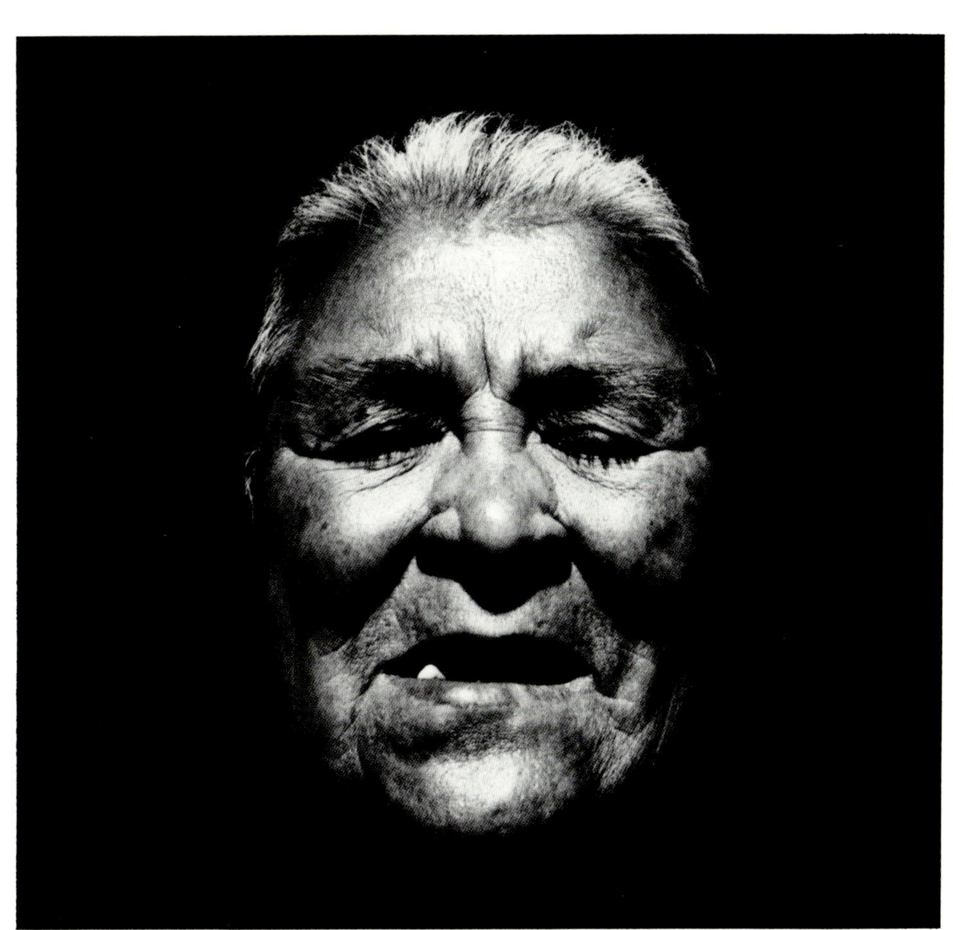

MR. JOHNSON

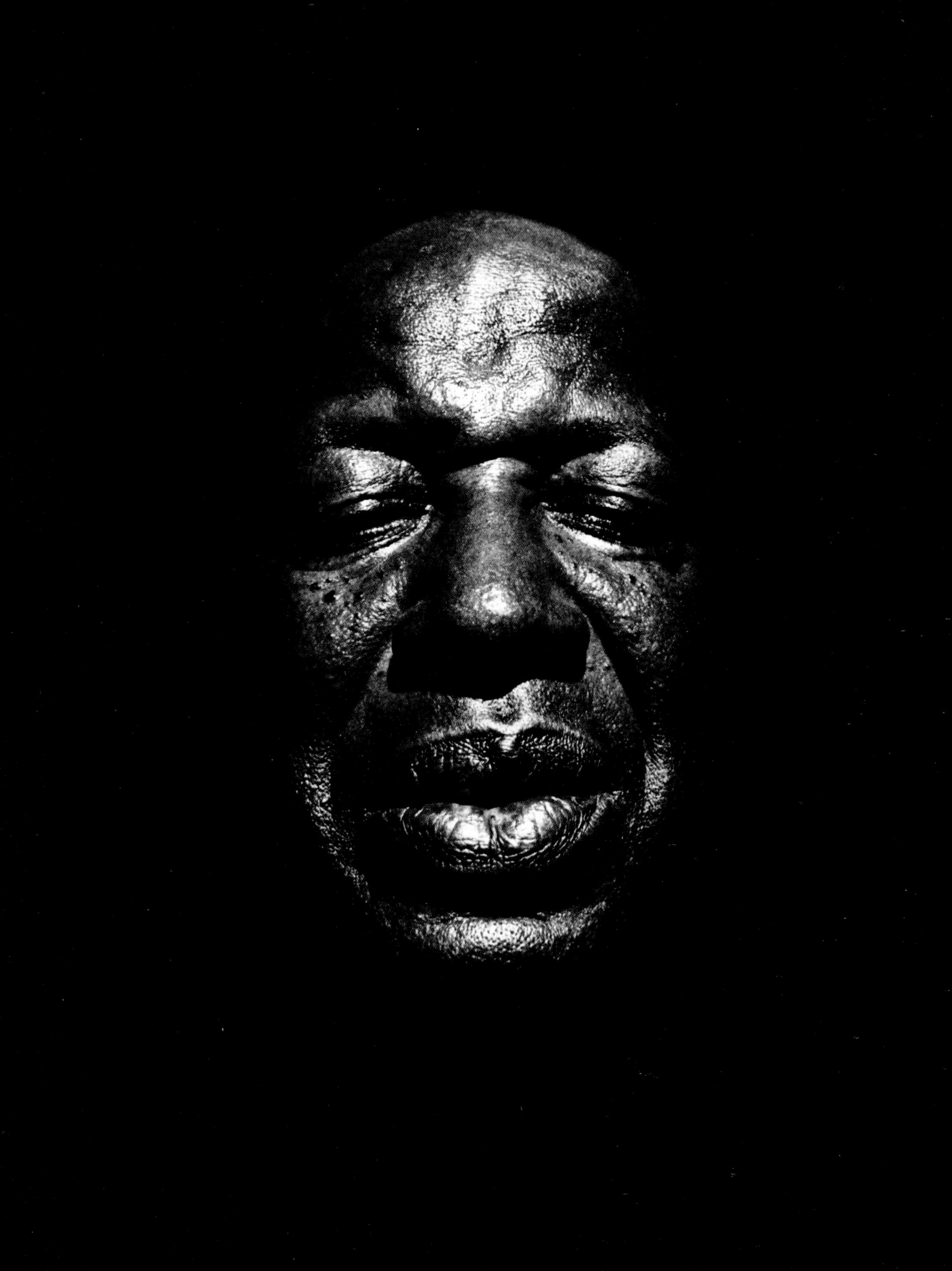

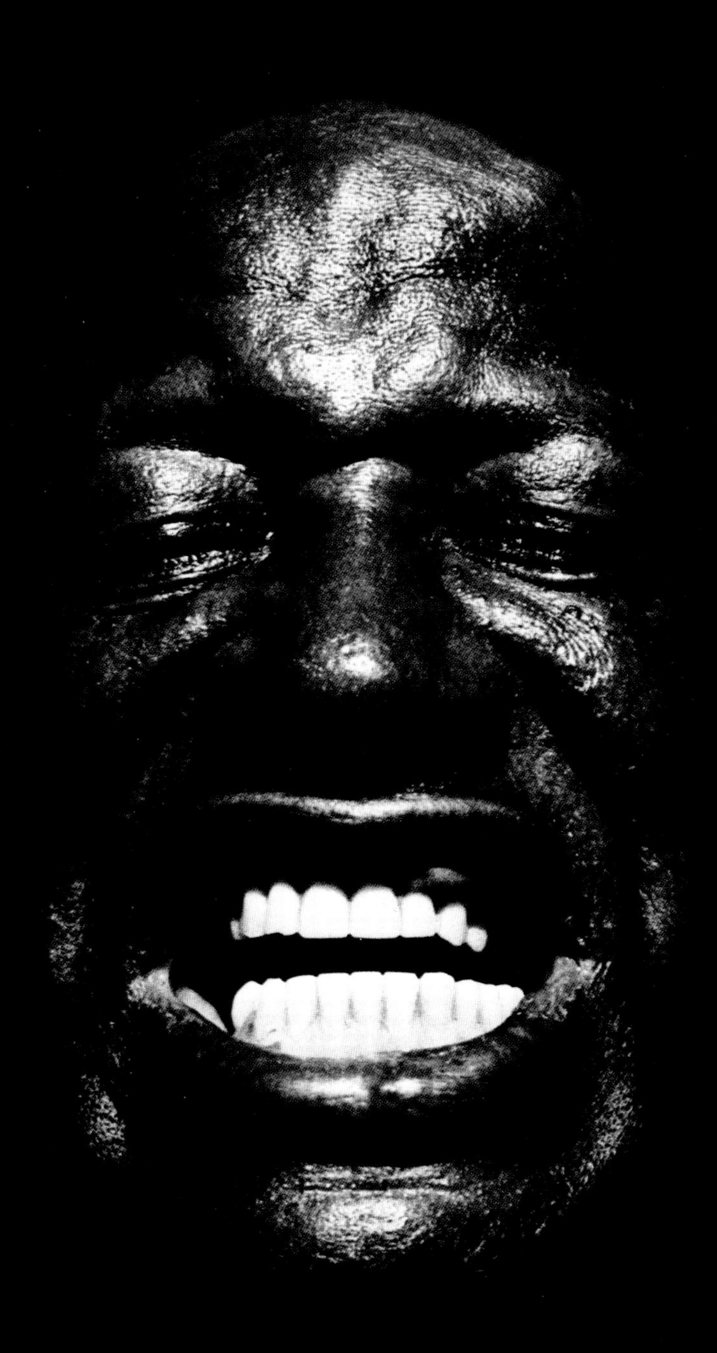

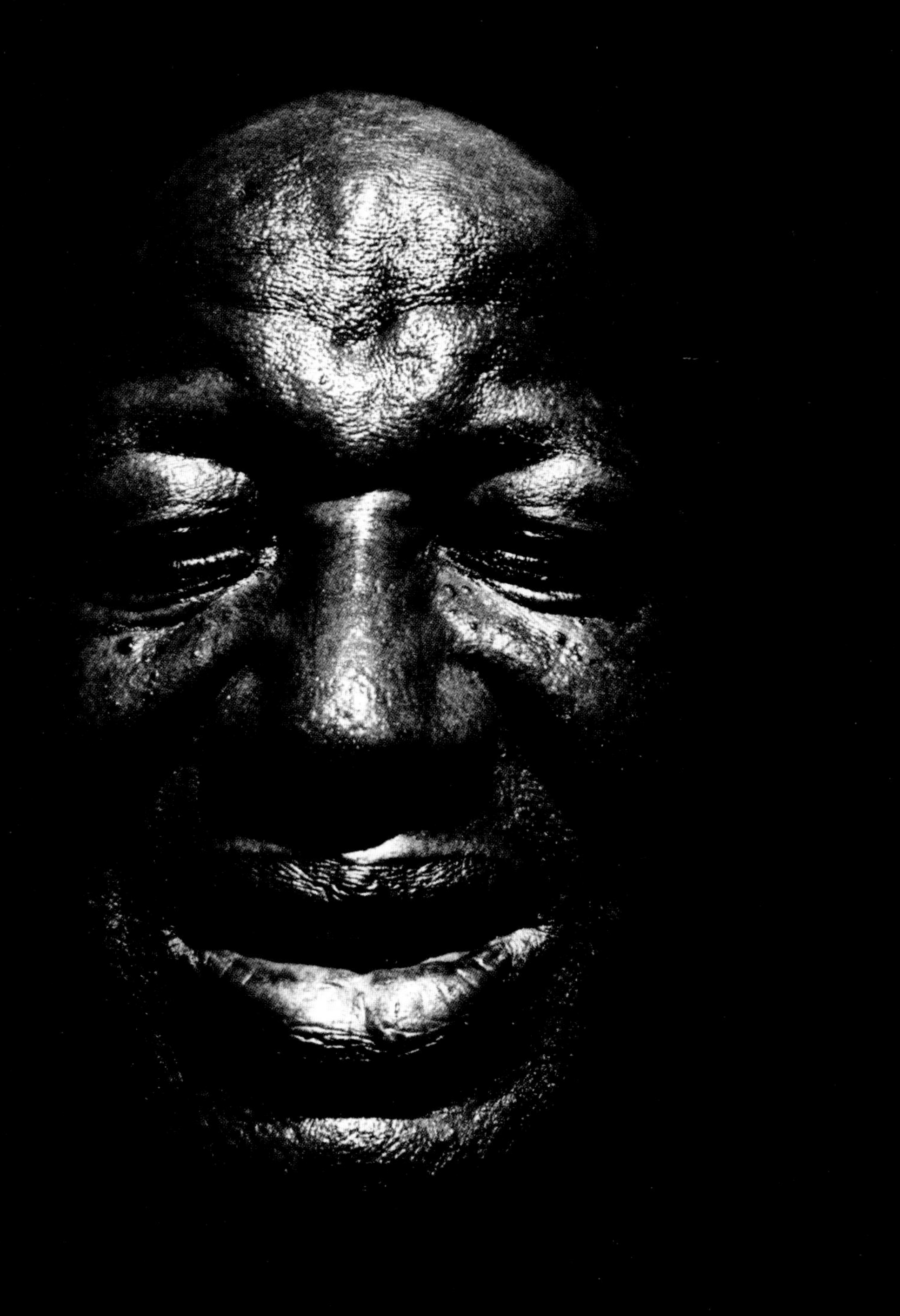

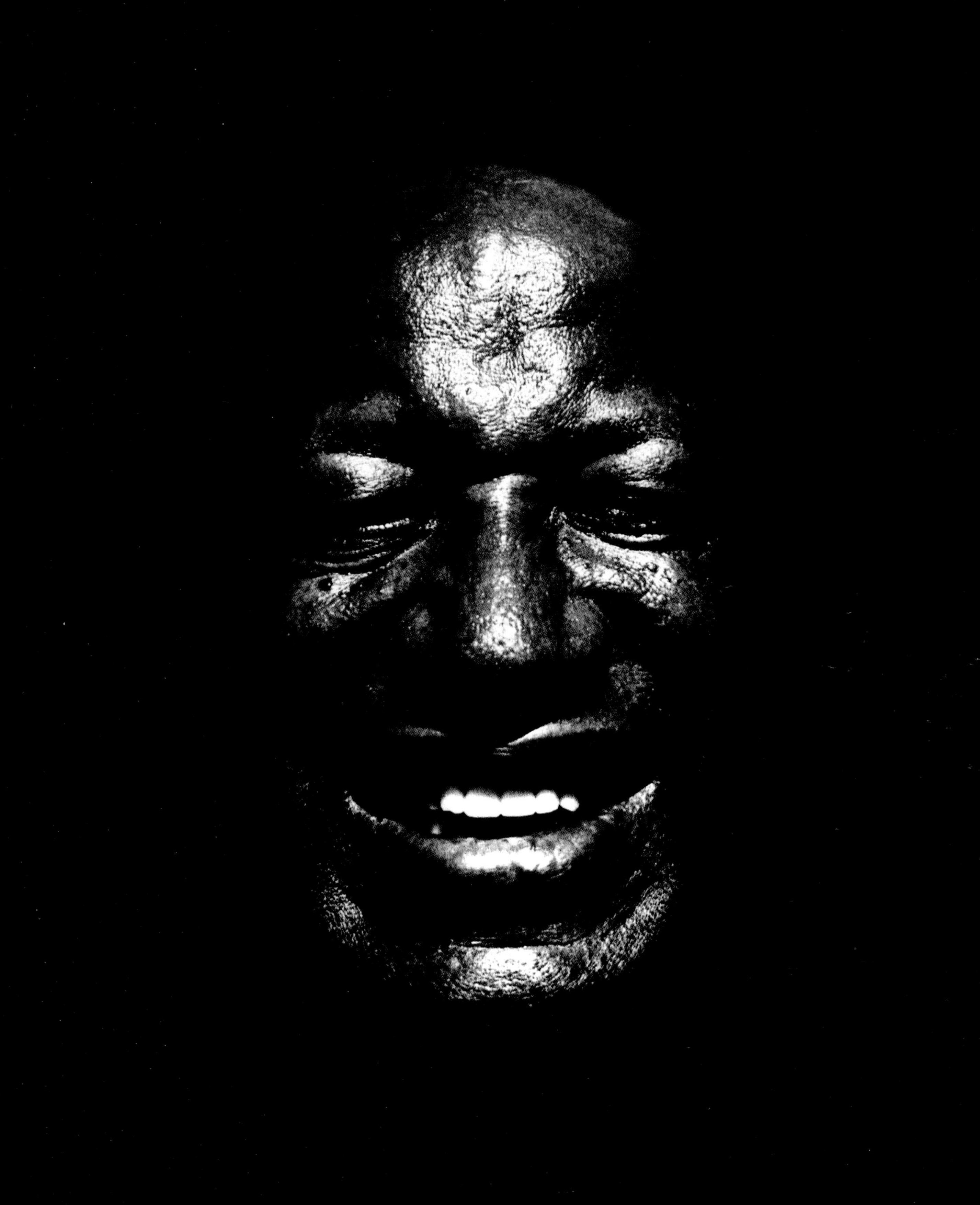

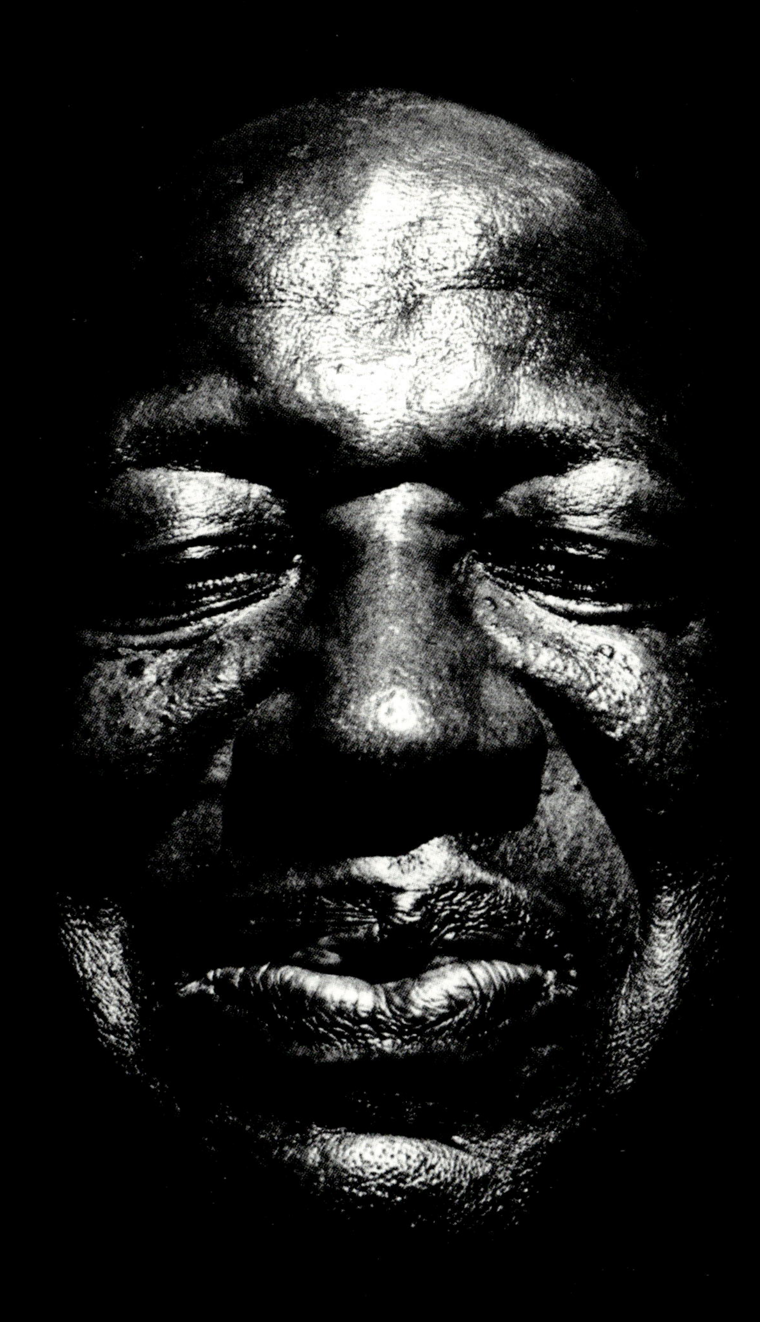

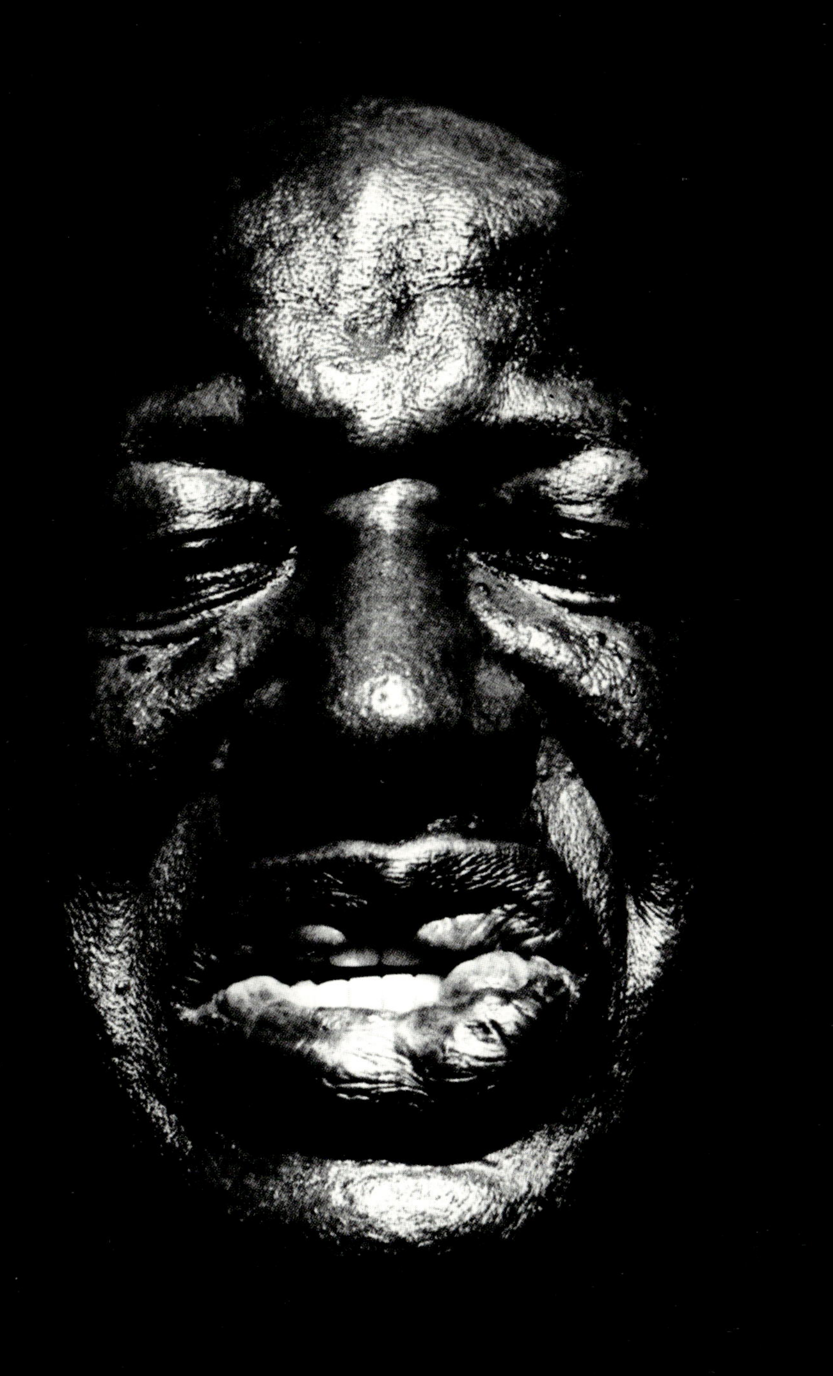

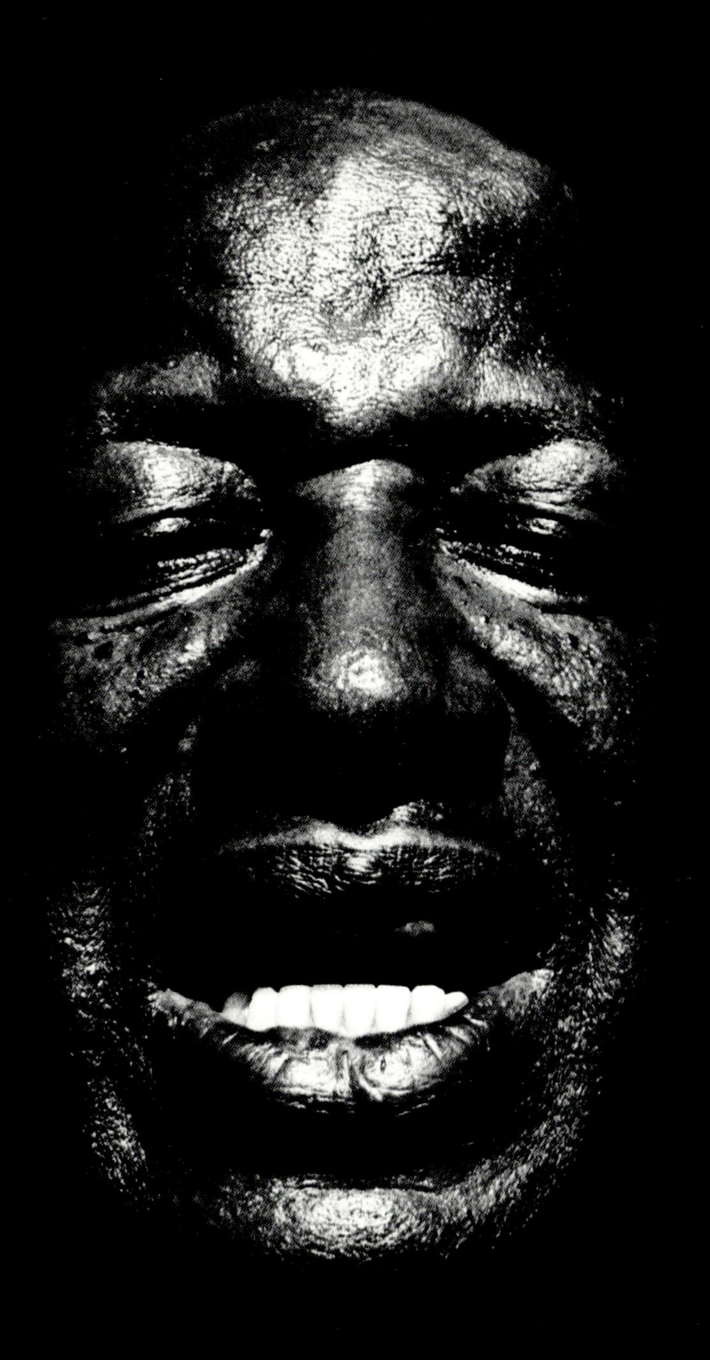

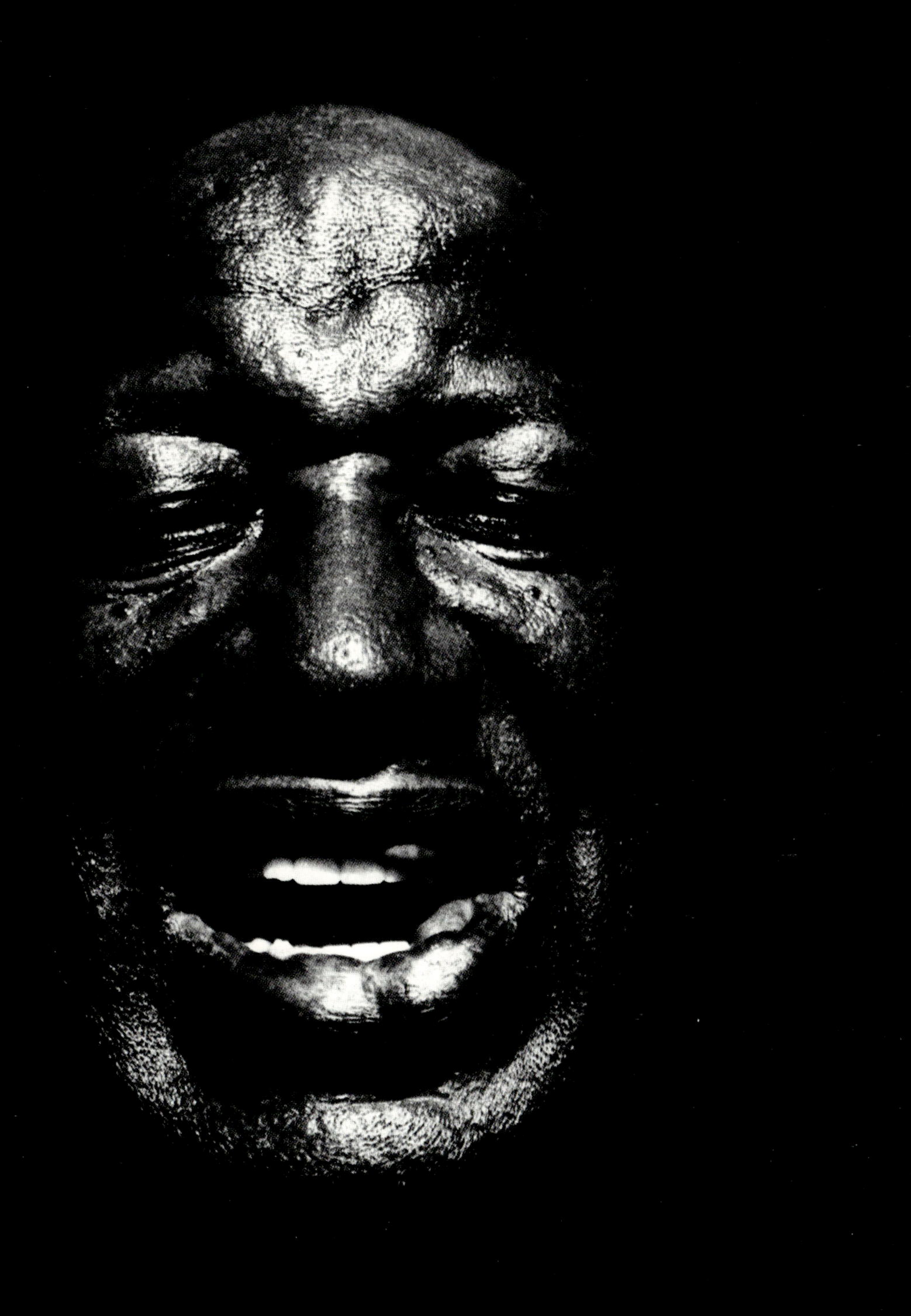